DATE DUE

DEMCO 38-296

Librarianship and the Information Paradigm

Richard Apostle
and
Boris Raymond

The Scarecrow Press, Inc.
Lanham, Md., & London
1997

SCARECROW PRESS, INC.

Published in the United States of America
by Scarecrow Press, Inc.
4720 Boston Way
Lanham, Maryland 20706

4 Pleydell Gardens, Folkestone
Kent CT20 2DN, England

British Library Cataloguing in Publication Information Available

Library of Congress Cataloging-in-Publication Data

Apostle, Richard A.
    Librarianship and the information paradigm / Richard Apostle and
Boris Raymond.
        p.   cm.
    Includes bibliographical references and index.
    ISBN 0–8108–3273–9
        1. Library science—Canada.   2. Information science—Canada.
I. Raymond, Boris, 1925–   . II. Title.
Z665. 2. C2A66   1997
020' . 971—dc21
                                                          96–40043
                                                              CIP

ISBN 0–8108–3273–9 (cloth : alk. paper)

CONTENTS

TABLES

PREFACE

This book began as a series of casual conversations at Dalhousie University's Graduate House over a decade ago. Boris Raymond was then a member of the School of Library and Information Studies at Dalhousie University and Richard Apostle was (and is) a member of the university's Sociology and Social Anthropology Department. Raymond was much involved in the ongoing debates about appropriate curriculum or new technologies for a small professional unit; Apostle was teaching and doing research on postindustrial systems. It quickly became evident that sociological work, particularly Daniel Bell's occupied a central position in the professional disputes. Further, the professional debates, given their concern for communication and information technologies, touched on major controversies about the possible emergence of postindustrial economies and postmodern cultures.

The fact that both of us are graduates of the University of California at Berkeley in sociology facilitated the creation of common intellectual perspectives on the analysis of professional groups. Our shared pedigree as graduands of the coffee houses of northern California means that we needed few excuses to meet and possibly discuss yet another project at this fascinating intersection of academic and professional literature.

We first worked our way cautiously through the labour market studies that have been adapted for this book (chapters 5 and 6), as well as some others (Apostle, Raymond, and Smith, 1984; Apostle and Raymond, 1986; Duffy, Raymond, and Apostle, 1989), before branching out to look at the related topics examined in other chapters. The interest some of our original work sparked encouraged us to expand the scope of our research topics. The debates, if anything, have intensified, and we hope we have made a contribution to them. Unless otherwise specified, the work here has been jointly done by Apostle and Raymond.

INTRODUCTION

This is a study of libraries and the library profession, and how they have been affected by the paradigmatic conflict of the last two decades; it is not a study of modern society as a whole, or of the nature of social communications, the computer industry, or entropy. Two conflicting paradigms, the Library Service and the Information paradigms, are competing for acceptance by the professional library community in Great Britain and North America. On the outcome of this competition depend the future content of library education, the choice of emphasized professional activities and skills, the types of services that will be provided and the sections of the public that will be served, as well as many other aspects of existing library institutions

Professional literature on the issues involved is vast indeed, but most of it is based on personal assertions, quotations from authorities, and deductions from abstract notions about the nature of post-industrial society. Our approach will be different. We shall be focusing primarily on libraries as organizations and upon librarians as professionals and not, as many other studies have done, on the nature of societal communications, linguistic codes, expert systems, or computer and electronic communications (the so-called information technology). Nor did we anticipate that our empirical findings, limited as they were by financial and time constraints, would result in any final "proofs" relating to the matters under investigation. Rather, it was our expectation that the results obtained would provide a general indication of probability of this or that hypothesis.

Our research and analysis will be presented here in logical, rather than chronological, order. Boris Raymond begins by discussing the current debates about information science and librarianship as a conflict between competing paradigms for the (re)organization of a professional field. We then move, in chapter 2, to an examination of the current work conditions that prevail in the world of Canadian librarianship. This second chapter will establish a useful benchmark for considering the dimensions of a professional domain, as well as the prospects for changing it. In chapters 3 and 4, we examine two key areas for indications of conflict and overlap between potentially different professional domains. In chapter 3, we look at the comparative history of the two major institutional codifications of professional wisdom in the world of Canadian librarianship — the National Library and the Canada Institute for Scientific and Technical Information (CISTI). The similarities, and differences, should help us assess the institutional commitments condition and delimit organizational alternatives. In chapter 4, we evaluate the current convergences and divergences in the pertinent professional literature. Using a selected group of relevant journals, we use journal titles and abstracts, as well as other data, to study the elements that separate, and potentially bind, two reasonably distinct intellectual worlds.

In chapters 5 and 6, we report on our earlier research on labour market conditions. Simply put, chapter 5 represents an exploration of the specific demands that exist for professional expertise in Canadian librarianship, while chapter 6 investigates the capacity of the profession to supply professional expertise. The seventh chapter turns to the structure and curriculum of Canada's seven graduate schools for library and information science. We study the evolution of core curriculum for these units and discuss some related institutional developments. In the concluding chapter, Richard Apostle summarizes the basic empirical patterns that have been identified and discusses the practical and theoretical significance of the findings.

We are indebted to the Social Science and Humanities Research Council of Canada for its continuing support of our endeavours. We are grateful for the grant (809-91-0007) that permitted us to do the projects discussed in chapters 2, 3, 4, and 7, as well as an earlier grant (410-87-0523) to investigate the labour market problems that stimulated this larger work. Among the many individuals who have participated in our projects we particularly wish to thank the members of Canada's library and information schools for sharing time and wisdom with us. We have listed these individuals and their institutional affiliations on page 122. We also acknowledge the following for reading portions of the manuscript: William Birdsall, Michael Buckland, Roma Harris, Norman Horrocks, Oriel MacLennan, and Lindy Siegert.

We are also indebted to the Survey Centre at the Gorsebrook Research Institute for providing an invaluable institutional base for our survey studies (chapters 2, 5, and 6). We especially thank Madine VanderPlaat, the centre's director, and Daphne Tucker for their assistance. We enjoyed working with Kim Adams on chapter 3, and Paul Smith on Chapter 4. Their respective backgrounds in librarianship and sociological methodology enriched our studies. Major appreciation goes to Donna Edwards. Her organizational and financial skills were crucial to the data collection stages of the various projects. She also handled the idiosyncratic drafting practices of the authors with ease, and prepared the final version of the manuscript.

CHAPTER 1

PARADIGMS IN CONFLICT
(by Boris Raymond)

Today, two seemingly incompatible perspectives are contending for the soul of librarianship. The first, known as the Library Service paradigm, is typified by the 1982 assertion of Daniel Boorstin, former Librarian of Congress, "the autonomous reader is the be-all and end-all of our libraries" (Boorstin, 1982: 1379). The second, often referred to as the Information paradigm, is distinguished by a focus on libraries as providers of "information."[1]

The original formulation of the functions of libraries was built around the activities of collecting, organizing, preserving, and circulating texts, in addition to providing a variety of auxiliary services to library users. The alternate interpretation of the role of libraries that has emerged in the last three decades consists of a cluster of assumptions regarding the process of informing users with the aid of powerful new electronic (computer) technology. Its roots go back to the second half of the nineteenth century. They were a by-product of a major growth in scientific and industrial research, a growth that gave rise to an unprecedented need for the provision of immediate factual as well as bibliographic data to selected groups of users. It also gave rise to the emergence of information centers[2] and technical libraries that could provide access to specialized material and data required by their clientele.

The two conceptions of librarianship gradually diverged, and by the 1970s they were actively competing with each other for the right to define the nature of the library profession. The four principal arenas within which the conflict is currently taking place are the library press, the Internet, the professional library associations, and the university-based library schools, many now renamed schools of library and information science (or study), LIS for short. The impact of the conflict on library institutions cannot be exaggerated. Will libraries continue to serve the public's broad educational, cultural and recreational needs, or will future librarians consider such needs peripheral and outside their professional concerns? Will all libraries be transformed into appendages of the scientific, technical and business establishment? Will the distinction between librarianship and "information management" disappear? Will predictions about the proximate end of libraries be accomplished by librarians who have become converts to the Information paradigm? There can be little doubt that acceptance of the Information paradigm's vision of libraries entails a number of serious implications for the library profession as a whole. Among these will be a major reorientation of library education, and of the public relations priorities of professional associations. Another will be a major reorientation from service to the general reader, to schoolchildren, and to those who cannot afford to purchase the books they need, to commercial, technical, and research interests.

Deliberately formulated theories in librarianship, as in all fields, contain two distinguishable elements: hypotheses based upon generalizations derived from systematic observation and background assumptions that have not been explicitly stated. Assumptions may be derived from personal experiences, collective definitions propounded by authorities, class interests, and from indoctrination by special interest groups. While they differ from systematically gathered "facts," such perspectives are nevertheless experienced with intensity by their adherents and eventually became components of interlocking generalizations about a particular phenomena. Paradigms play a major role in the way events are interpreted by providing models that help assimilate new experiences. When, as a result of societal changes or scientific discoveries, the existing paradigm comes into conflict with a new reality, a different paradigm tends to emerge, one that helps create a new way of seeing the world, and provides a new vocabulary. Such has been the case with the emerging Information paradigm, which has attempted to impose a novel vocabulary on the old Library Service vocabulary: "professional information manager"[3] for librarian, and "information" for print-on-paper texts.

However, a new paradigm does not necessarily have to absorb the old one. Quite frequently the structure that underlies the new paradigm does not replace the old one but rather, as in the partition of cells, develops an independent if parallel existence with the structure that has given it rise. That is the central thesis of this book.

The Library Service Paradigm

Ancient libraries appeared simultaneously with the invention of writing and the collection of texts written on various materials. Originally libraries were virtually indistinguishable from archives.[4] The mission of the most famous library of antiquity, that of Alexandrian library, was "to collect every book written in Greek as well as the sacred and famous works of people outside of the OIKUMENE" and to provide research facilities to scholars (Wellisch, 1994: 19). In ancient Greece and Rome, libraries were often attached to temples and served as archival depositories for the priesthood. Other libraries were open to the public and provided texts that private individuals could not afford to purchase for themselves.

During the medieval period in Europe, libraries were most often found in monasteries or attached to cathedrals. Their primary function was that of storing potentially informative texts that could be borrowed by designated categories of individuals: monks, churchmen, or religious organizations. With the coming of the Renaissance and an increase in secular literacy, libraries began to appear in princely courts, in universities, and even in the private homes of the wealthy. Their function remained primarily that of the orderly storage and preservation of texts.

Not until the dawn of the modern era does one find a significant addition to the custodial role of libraries. Martin Luther advocated, for the saving of souls, that "no effort or expense should be spared to provide good libraries or book repositories, especially in the larger cities which can well afford them" (Jackson, 1974: 113). In England, by the middle of the nineteenth century, book collections had become accessible not only to the limited audience of the clergy, but also to literate parishioners. The use of privately owned libraries for the encouragement of religious and moral education was an accepted practice. The underlying conviction among promoters of such collections was that the reading of uplifting books would be a powerful tool in the hand of the virtuous; books could be used to improve the moral and educational level of the population and to spread useful knowledge among the lower classes. A similar belief lay behind the establishment of publicly funded libraries in the middle of the nineteenth century.

In the United States the middle of the nineteenth century saw the educational, cultural, and socializing role of libraries becoming widely accepted. Their ability to perform these functions was greatly expanded by the donations of Andrew Carnegie, who was a believer in the importance of libraries as the "peoples' universities."

> By the early 19th century nearly all of the settled regions of America had experimented with various forms of the "public" library — all designed to make books and other reading material more readily available to an ever increasing number of readers. (Harris, 1984: 189)

The need for a literate industrial workforce, as well as the necessity to acculturate the flood of foreign-born immigrants with a common American culture and sense of nationality created an additional task for libraries. In order to emphasize the public library's ability to participate in popular education, the Boston Public Library issued a policy statement that embodied the essence of the Library Service paradigm: the future of a democratic republic was made directly dependent upon the education of its citizenry. The public library was to be one of the principal constituents of the educational system.

> Reading ought to be furnished to all, as a matter of public policy and duty, on the same principle that we furnish free education ... the largest possible number of persons should be induced to read and understand questions going down to the very foundations of social order.... (Harris, 1984: 226)

Increasingly, however, the didactic overtones of such a formulation came to be questioned by librarians. By the 1930s dissatisfaction with the prescriptive role led to a revision of the mission of libraries, and to the abandonment of claims to special moral powers. Librarians now began to define themselves as expert guides who could help clients locate the most suitable texts on matters that interested them (Readers" Advisory or R.A.).

Today, there are more than seventeen thousand public libraries in North America, with over fifteen thousand in the United States and over seventeen hundred in Canada (*American Library Directory*, 1995: 443-446). They employ many thousands of professional librarians and act as community learning centers, community research and reference resources that support formal educational institutions, independent learning centers, and recreation centers. In terms of larger social purpose, libraries perform such socially necessary functions as encouraging reading, literacy and the diffusion of commonly-held cultural values. The Library Service paradigm reflects the above-listed functions, while recognizing that the function of conserving the total graphic record of mankind (texts, images, and the like) is primarily the responsibility of the major national, regional and university libraries, and that the function of informing clearly defined groups of special users is the domain of information centers and of some special libraries.

Criticisms leveled against the Library Service paradigm center on the contention that by not focusing on the "information" needs of individuals in postindustrial society, the paradigm has caused other professions to infringe upon "the library's turf." Critics also prophesy that the custodial function of libraries will soon be made redundant by electronic-based technology, which is far more efficient in processing "information" than the old-fashioned library with its print-on-paper technology. Others contend that the Library Service paradigm is too focused on the library as an institution, rather than on the "information" needs of people. They maintain that the majority of librarians are far too conservative, far too focused on their book collections, and not pro-active enough. Such characteristics, they contend, deprive librarians of prescriptive authority possessed by such professionals as doctors, leaving them bereft of status and with their image closer to that of clerks than of other professionals. As a result, librarians are unable to achieve decent career advancement, high income, and warranted social status. A further claim is that librarians have allowed themselves to become increasingly redundant in today's "information society," and are therefore being marginalized and doomed to extinction. The only solution, so the proponents of the Information paradigm argue, is for librarians to accept the necessity of becoming "professional information managers."

The Information Paradigm

As has been already noted, a new and different library clientele with a need for specific factual data, rather than for general cultural enlightenment, began to emerge in the last quarter of the nineteenth century. The clientele consisted mainly of engineers, managers, technologists, businessmen, government officials, and scientists. Their work required information centers and special libraries that contained primarily technical and other narrowly defined collections. Clients as a rule, were restricted to small groups of designated individuals. In the United States the basic commonality of information centers and special libraries was affirmed through the formation of the Special Libraries Association in 1909. From the very beginning, this organization considered its work to be distinct from that of public libraries. Special libraries were already being referred to as information bureaus in 1915. The main function of the general library is to make books available. The function of the special library is to make information available (Johnson, 1915: 158-159). Closely allied to, and encompassing the field of special librarianship was the documentation movement. The American Documentation Institute, which was organized in 1937, enlarged its activities during World War II, and by the middle of the 1960s it was renamed the American Society for Information Science. The expansion of military and industrial technology during and after World War II greatly intensified the dependence of science and industry upon retrieval of potentially informative texts (PITs) from a rapidly accumulating worldwide mass of specialized publications. The technical and scientific revolution emphasized the value of research to corporations, governments, and industry. As a result, information centers and special libraries became a common feature of industrial, business, and government agencies (Harris, 1984: 263-264). These organizations were faced with the near-impossible task of handling huge amounts of scientific and technical texts that were being produced around the world. They responded to this challenge by increasingly relying on improved technology. Fremont Rider's advocacy of microform technology, the experimentation with perforated IBM cards, and the introduction of new indexing systems were all attempts to satisfy the growing demand for effective retrieval of bibliographic and factual material.

At this point, in the middle 1960s, computer technology achieved a level of efficiency that made it cost-effective for handling massive bibliographic data such as Machine Readable Cataloguing (MARC). The advent of a new and extremely powerful technology qualitatively transformed library housekeeping, and changed the work of information centers and of those special libraries associated with scientific, industrial or technical work into what has been referred to as "hightech special libraries." As well, by giving their professional personnel control of a set of highly technical retrieval skills, the basis was laid for claiming a new professional designation — that of the "professional information manager." Developments also led to the reevaluation of theoretical assumptions that underlay the work of information centers and "hightech" special libraries, and prepared the ground for the emergence of the Information paradigm, whose formulation was greatly accelerated when a series of new theoretical constructs appeared in the writings of Bell, Licklider, and Lancaster. The writings of all three contained early statements of such key notions as "information society," "information retrieval" and "paperless society." These progenitors of the Information paradigm helped elaborate a new interpretation of the technological innovations in librarianship. Many of the paradigm's postulates rest on Bell's assertion that the advent of a post-industrial society meant that theoretical knowledge would become "the strategic resource, the axial principle" for a qualitatively new social structure. According to him, while industrial society had been based on machine technology, postindustrial society rested on intellectual technology — "information" — something that librarians could claim as their very own "turf." "The idea of the emergence of an information economy very rapidly caught on in the mass media, where it has been endowed with many meanings and treated and maltreated" (Crawford, 1983: 382).

Licklider considered books and other print-on-paper texts as inadequate depositories of "information," labeling them expensive and difficult to process rapidly. He stressed the need for a more efficient interaction between the "information" seeker and the "information" container (Birdsall, 1994: 16). For Licklider, books were too heavy, too expensive, and their circulation was too slow. For Lancaster the proximate paperless society was one in which communication technology, combined with computers, would displace paper systems, thus rendering libraries obsolete and mandating the transformation of librarians into "information professionals" (Harris and Hannah, 1994: 39).

In the years since the two authors initiated their critique of the Library Service paradigm, the movement to supplant it with a new formulation, one based on the concept of "information," has gradually crystallized. The new paradigm's prescription for librarianship is based on the central assumption that the function of libraries is the transmission of "information." In the most elementary form, the Information paradigm's message is simplicity itself: since everything that libraries handle is "information," library and "information" work are one and the same thing. And while the Information paradigm has not yet gained total acceptance by librarians, any reading of the current library literature will show that its major premises hold wide credence. Those librarians working in information centers and "hightech", special libraries, as well as many LIS faculty members, are especially prone to accept the new paradigm.*

Today, the mature Information paradigm rests on the following eight key assumptions, only some of which have been stated explicitly, and none of which has as yet been subjected to an in-depth analysis:

1. "information" is the basic concept upon which the paradigm rests;
2. postindustrial societies are "information societies";
3. a merger of library and information sciences is taking place;
4. "information technology" is the driving force and the determiner of the future functions of libraries and of the "information profession";
5. the needs of library users and the functions of libraries need to be reformulated in terms of "information needs";
6. the concepts "information industry" and "information profession" are interdependent;
7. a convergence of library and information science education is necessary and inevitable;
8. employment prospects for LIS graduates in the "emerging information market" are optimistic.

The positive characteristics attributed to the Information paradigm are that its theoretical formulation places science, business, and technology in the forefront, and that it is congruent with rapidly evolving "information technology." The paradigm also provides a basis for theoretical research and a theoretical discipline that universities today require from their academic units.   It thus gives "information professionals" a theoretical focus, at the same time; it places them in the center of today's technological developments.

Were it not for attempts by adherents of the Information paradigm to absorb the whole of librarianship, there would be no need to subject the above assumptions to an in-depth critique. Indeed, the paradigm's treatment of the process by which technical and scientific knowledge is

---

*   For an analysis of the motivation involved, see the section entitled "Qui Bono," pp. 129-132 in chapter 8.

retrieved is both apposite and comprehensive, and is a welcome contribution. Unfortunately, some enthusiasts have attempted to extend its generalizations into territory which has only a remote relation to "information" work. Such intellectual imperialism requires a critical evaluation.

The Information Concept

"Information" is the central concept of the Information paradigm and is pivotal to the attempt to redefine the library profession; all formulations of the paradigm are based on this concept.

"Information" is a polysemous term, one which may be pronounced and spelled identically, but has multiple referents. Lewis Carroll called such words "portmanteau words," in order to underline the multitude of their meanings. In the past, for librarians, "information" was associated primarily with the process of informing their users about the content or the location of books and other similar artifacts, and of providing needed bibliographical data. "Information" has also been used to designate any set of data, events, or names that are compiled according to some stipulated organizational scheme. Today the term is used to designate everything under the sun, including all texts that a library may contain. The term is habitually used to signify knowledge, the process of becoming informed, and the carrier of human communications, as well as to refer to data, facts, and different types of "information" such as bibliographic, statistical, or any research results. It is frequently used as an adjective to modify general nouns such as "information professionals," "information society," and "information environment." Employment of the term in other than library contexts covers the function of genetic structures, current news relating to political, economic, and sporting events, and technical/scientific data within a particular discipline. Another meaning attached to the term relates to intelligence-gathering activities. In current computer science and business literature, "information" is almost always associated with computer manipulation of arrays of data; any text that can be manipulated by computer is called "information." Thus, by a gradual process of verbal osmosis, anything at all that is handled by computers (themselves arbitrarily labeled "information technology"), becomes "information," tout simple. In short, even the briefest perusal of current library literature shows that "information" is constantly used in different ways, and often within a single paragraph.

Such misusage of the word is not devoid of serious problems. Our understanding of social reality is shaped, in large measure, by perceptual categories, and language plays a major role in the formation of these categories. Confusion with regard to the meaning of key terms inevitably obscures important issues. Words do more than convey meaning (i.e., denote signifiers such as objects, texts, thoughts, events). They also convey (connote) emotional associations, (i.e., feelings of good and bad, prestige, status). Words with such broad meanings as to make it impossible either to agree or disagree with their usage are especially prone to cause confusion. Many years ago Alice, in Lewis Carroll's classic *Through the Looking-Glass*, is said to have pointed out the problem caused by the imprecise use of words when she responded to Humpty Dumpty's assertion that, "When *I* use a word, it means just what I choose it to mean — neither more nor less." To which arrogant declaration Alice replied, "The question is, whether you *can* make words mean so many different things."

Effective scholarly communication presupposes that the words used will have clear and specifiable referents. No effective dialogue can be sustained when the key terms used are so vague, or so general, that it is possible to interpret them in any way one pleases, notwithstanding Humpty Dumpty's assertion of his prerogative to do so. One must, of course, recognize the value of legitimate forms of abstraction in the use of concepts. The present critique, however, focuses on the less legitimate practice by which individuals seek to obfuscate issues through the use of concepts which are uncircumscribed in their denotation. Far from being a peripheral academic fuss over recondite meanings, the use and misuse of the "I" word have led to misleading, manipulative, and, at times, truly bizarre assertions. Its constant misuse lies at the root of the misunderstanding between supporters of the Library Service and the Information paradigms.

The problem with misusing the term is that such practice obscures, and often obliterates, important distinctions between what skills spies, computer scientists, accountants, and librarians require. The multiple referents of the term allow individuals to transfer the attributes possessed by one usage of a term to a totally different signification of the same term. Thus, for example, the term "health professional" may refer to an orderly, a laboratory technician, a nurse, a general practitioner, or a heart transplant surgeon. By failing to specify that one is referring to an orderly, one can mislead an audience into attributing the status of a heart surgeon to an orderly.

"Information" in the original Latin root means a process to communicate or something to be communicated to someone (Yuexiao, 1983: 480) and does not refer to the container that carries the message (book, text, scroll, or electronic disk), nor does it refer to knowledge, to genetic codes, rules of grammar, organized data, or some "metaessence" — all meanings currently assigned to the term. While "information" has been defined in a large number of different ways in current library literature, there is no one meaning on which its numerous users agree. As Buckland wrote, "It is ironic that the term "information" is itself ambiguous and used in different ways" (Buckland, 1991: 3-4).

In an attempt to bring some measure of order into the chaos and to reduce semantic uncertainty by clustering the various usages, Buckland has created a seminal classification that differentiates these usages into three distinct categories: "information-as-process," when someone is being informed, when what they know is being changed; "information-as-knowledge," knowledge that has been communicated; and "information-as-thing," when the term "information is also used attributively for objects, such as data and documents, that are referred to as information because they are regarded as being informative" (Buckland, 1991: 3).

In the drive for greater inclusion through abstraction, concepts like "information" begin to lose their concrete denotation, while retaining the full power of connotation. The more abstract they are, the more diffuse their meanings become. Such concepts come to have a broad generality, but at a price; the meaning of things they communicate is leveled. Originating in Shannon's mathematical abstractions, the Information paradigm treated all "information" as an undifferentiated phenomenon and did not differentiate between such types of "information" as bibliographic, statistical, current news, weather report, community event, and espionage. There is also the loss of specificity caused by the fact that there are many types of skills involved in "information" work, from knowledge about where a particular book is located in a library (bibliographic knowledge), to the ability to analyze espionage data (intelligence analysis), or the evaluation of the credit rating of a construction firm (financial analysis). Evidently, different types of "information" work have to be handled by distinct professions.

The notion that all text-containing artifacts in a library are "information" is nonsense. Messages or texts are not "information" until they have informed someone. At most they may be considered as "potentially informative texts" (PITs). Since we know that many texts are, for one reason or another, not informative, we can be certain that they are not all "information." A text is not informative if written in an unknown language, or if on a subject that the reader cannot understand (Einstein's mathematics, for example), or already known to the reader, or if a reader rejects its message on ideological or religious grounds. There cannot be uninformative "information." Such a notion is clearly a logical absurdity[5] and it is clearly incorrect, even semantically manipulative, to employ the same term to designate two contradictory phenomena, even if, as some insist, language is as it is used.

The term's ambiguity is largely based on semantic confusion. Questions can legitimately arise as to whether the same thing, or several different things, is being referred to by such a term. A second cause of confusion is the fact that different disciplines often use the same term to designate quite different referents, with each discipline assuming that its particular usage is the universal one. A third problem is that general' terms such as "transportation," or "information," represent high levels of abstraction, and the higher the order of abstraction, the more their specific meaning is lost. The process of abstracting, of leaving specific characteristics out, while it is an indispensible convenience for day-to-day conversation, presents real hazards to scholarly communication. Transportation loses the distinction between jet planes and bicycles; an expert bibliographer and an accountant both become "information professionals," communication becomes imprecise; obfuscation reigns. Once one admits the legitimacy of applying the term "information" to a thing, to an object — book or text — then the whole material universe becomes "information." Hardly a useful thing to do.

There is an extensive, if largely ignored, body of scholarly thought that questions the semantic perturbations associated with the use and misuse of the "information" concept. According to Canadian LIS professor Schrader, "the term 'information' is fuzzy and elicits dissensus rather than consensus in the scholarly community" (Schrader, 1984: 249). Another academic critic, California philosophy professor Theodore Roszak, writing in 1986, exclaimed that the word "information" has become the god-word of our time (Roszak, 1986: 19). As long ago as 1972 Hans Wellisch identified thirty-nine different definitions of "information science" extant in literature between 1959 and 1971 (Wellisch, 1972: 170-171). He concluded that the concept had no generally accepted definition, was highly ambiguous and used sometimes by people who had only a very dim idea of what they were talking about but were happy to have a vogue word which could be bandied around freely" (Wellisch, 1972: 160). Fritz Machlup, the pioneer student of the economics of knowledge, has also strongly objected to the misuse of the concept (Machlup, 1980: 205-206).

The confusion inherent in this overused and misused term presents a major obstacle to any rational analysis of the role of libraries and librarians because the term permits the introduction of false propositions about the role of books, libraries, and librarians in a manner that is not immediately obvious to an average audience. An instance of this was the American Library Association's recent claim that "information delivery" should be the "turf" of libraries, on the grounds that libraries have been handling "information" for over one hundred years, whereas in fact, libraries through this period handled only a small fraction of all informative materials, primarily books and periodicals. They most certainly did not handle orally transmitted "information," in-house analyses of the financial position of a business, countless church sermons, classroom lectures, informative personal letters, and endless other instances of informative activity. Such overweening claims are easily seen through by individuals outside the library profession, and go a long way toward mistakenly discrediting librarianship.

In day-to-day conversation, precision of understanding may not be crucial; one deduces meanings from their context. But when one is making predictions about the future of the library profession, or discussing future employment prospects with LIS students, using the term "information," without specifying what type of "information" work is being referred to, necessarily leads to a blurring of meaning and to faulty communication, if not to outright deception by an expansion of the meaning of the term. Such usage affects every aspect of professional library discourse: the nature of education for librarianship, the definition of the library profession, and its relationship with such professions as management, journalism, accounting, education, and computer science. The misuse of the term is conducive to an exaggeration of the scope and extent of the skills of librarians, and tends to obliterate the difference between various libraries and their functions. It helps create an artificial semantic cross-over between general library services and the highly specialized activity of information centers and "hightech" special libraries. Wholesale application of the term tends to blur the distinction between receiving communication in the form of literary fiction and an array of numerical data; an expert bibliographer and an accountant both become "information managers." An incunabulum becomes an "information" container; a poem by Byron is equated to an engineering formula. The problem of applying the term "information" to what Buckland calls "information-as thing," that is, to a book or a text, or any other physical representation of a communication, is that then it becomes a portmanteau word that denotes anything and everything in the universe, from a gene, to a manuscript, to Buckland's antelope — and thereby loses all meaning.

In summary, precise definitions, specificity, and nonambiguity are the sine qua non of effective scholarly communication. Overuse, careless use, semantic manipulation, and misplaced reification of the term "information" serve to create ambiguity and cause great harm to the library profession; the "information" concept is far too indeterminate to be useful in any serious discussion about the profession's present and future role.

Most of us are inclined to be careless in our communications with one another. Instead of using precise words to express ourselves, we fall into the habit of relying on shortcuts, stock phrases and cliches, saying "information" when we mean data, knowledge, facts, ideas, hunches, books, texts, or documents. Having lumped all these different referents under one portmanteau term, we often slide into the illusion that we are dealing with a single phenomenon when in fact we are dealing with a plurality. And, after we have repeated the process enough times, we begin using this by now totally ambiguous term to erect intellectual constructs built on sand. One would do well to remember that the word "information" is a set of sounds or graphic symbols. The existence of this sequence of symbols does not imply that they represent anything real in the objective world, any more than did such terms as phlogiston, angels, and hell. Like "evil" and "good," "information" is a reification of many different acts of informing, and is not made any more real by being transformed from a verb into a noun, for example, eating into "eatery," teaching into "teachery," informing into "information."

Assumption of an "Information Society"

The Information paradigm is also based on the proposition that postindustrial societies are "information societies" in which "information" is the central and most dynamic element. This implies that in postindustrial societies, technical and scientific knowledge and its dissemination play a qualitatively larger role than they did in traditional agricultural or industrial societies. Proponents of the paradigm assert that in postindustrial societies, professions that specialize in the transmission of "information" will achieve high status and high material rewards.

The negative impact of the "information society" assumption comes from a tendency to create a false identity between the roles of the vast majority of librarians and the few "professional information managers" who work in highly computerized information centers, in some research library departments, and in some special libraries. Thus an illusion is created that all libraries must become primarily providers of "information." Such an implication suggests that the present noninformation services of libraries, especially the public, school, and undergraduate college ones, must be either entirely abandoned or at the very least greatly diminished. The argument is further reinforced by predictions of the proximate demise of libraries, and by extravagant promises to those who are prepared to reconstitute themselves into "information managers."

Assumption Regarding the Merger of Library and Information Science

Another key assumption of the Information paradigm is that library science is currently merging with information science into a single discipline referred to as library/information science. Librarians are said to have a commonality of theoretical knowledge based upon the integration of library and information sciences. The assumed linkage has even given rise to a new lexicon: professionals working in libraries are now referred to as "information managers" on the grounds that they are not just custodians of books, but play a key role in the processing and provision of "information." Once again, this assumption rests on the misleading definition of libraries as "information" organizations. Such a "front-end-loaded" rhetorical device utilizes an arbitrary definition that, when accepted, renders the desired conclusion inevitable. In this case, once one accepts the assumption that library organizations are "information" institutions, it then has to follow that the science that studies their structure and function must of necessity be Information Science.

The second part of the merger assumption is the equation of computer-based library technology ("information technology") with

Information Science, and the tendency to see the increase in applications of "information technology" as the dominant aspect of current library developments. The assumption equates the priorities of information centers and some highly computerized special libraries with those of all libraries. While this chapter can not deal at length with the question whether "information science" is a legitimate concept, or a "house built on sand," (Vagianos, 1972a: 153), it is legitimate to note that librarianship does not constitute a single "science," but rather of a conglomerate of sciences, disparate techniques, practices, and ethical prescriptions, borrowed from a variety of sources such as chemistry — in paper and film conservation work, psychology — the impact of reading on the development of children or the impact of stereotypes, and computer science — the creation of systems and databases for on-line bibliographic files. Looking over the list, one is led to suspect that the term "library science" is merely an inappropriate translation of the German term *bibliothekswissenschaft*.

> The profession (Information Science) has no unique disciplinary base but draws whatever it finds useful from research anywhere in the bibliographic R & D sector and anywhere outside — sociology, management studies, communication, and other fields. (Wilson, 1983: 396)

The merger assumption is designed to reinterpret the content of librarianship in order to make the profession reflect the type of work performed by "information managers" in special libraries. This is accomplished by obscuring the substantial difference between the study of the processes of "information transfer" on the one hand, and the study of how best to provide library services to the general library user on the other.

Assumptions Regarding Information Technology

"Information technology" is considered by adherents of the Information paradigm as the fundamental factor that underlies all future library developments. Adherents of the Information paradigm argue that technology is the driving force that is transforming librarians into "professional information managers." Further changes in the technology, which are expected to be predictable, supposedly indicate that books and

other print-on-paper items are soon to be replaced by electronic signals.
As referred to by the paradigm's adherents, "information technology"
includes communications technology (optic fiber, regular wires, wireless,
and voice mail), as well as microfilm, fiche, CD-ROM storage, imaging
technology, and computers (Chen, 1992: 3). Actually, any technology
that informs individuals should be considered as "information"
technology, including the one based on the old-fashioned card catalogue.
However, because of the massive power of modern computers, and the
skillful advertising techniques of the computer industry, there exists
today a general tendency to identify "information technology" exclusively
with electronic-based technologies. Such a definition is congruent with
the paradigm's identification of all library functions with those performed
primarily only by "hightech" special libraries. For professionals working
in such organizations, extremely powerful computer and communications
technologies are indeed indispensible tools, with which they tend to
identify. And, it is certainly true that many of the changes occurring in
library work have come about due to computers. (The example of the
Library of Congress MARC cataloguing data well illustrates this fact.)
However, to identify most of the work of school, public, and
undergraduate college libraries with high-speed searches of massive
databases, bibliographic or otherwise, is to misrepresent completely the
central function of such libraries. While most libraries, along with
numerous other institutions, depend on computers for their data
processing and other housekeeping chores, it is indeed far-fetched to
identify these activities with their core functions. School, public and
undergraduate college libraries engage in a wide gamut of activities that
have little or nothing to do with providing "information," or with the
utilization of "information technology" (e.g. literacy training, teaching
children to learn to enjoy poetry, and providing students with texts they
need in order to write their essays).

Such glib over generalizations are both incorrect and harmful to
most librarians because they detract from the importance of their core
functions, forcing them to redefine themselves as information center
analysts. They also undermine the self-esteem of the very many librarians
who, as Roma Harris has argued so cogently, value their tradition of
service to the public, rather than be exclusively preoccupied with
technology (Harris, 1992). Many authors have questioned other aspects
of the assumptions concerning "information technology." They have
pointed out that far from being displaced by print-on-paper, books are
coming out in ever greater numbers.

> Book sales in the United States increased almost 16 percent in
> the first nine months of 1992 as compared to 1991. . . . Between
> April 1991 and March 1992, 822 million adult books were sold
> in the United States. (Crawford and Gorman, 1995: 16)

Many others have pointed out that the usefulness of printed materials
extends far beyond that of providing instant "information." In any case,
the many millions of books that are presently stored in libraries will not
be transformed into on-line electronic messages within the lifetime of
present professional librarians or of library users. Until the great classics
of literature, past periodical literature, and all other genres are made
available in digital format, the great mass of library users — rich and
poor alike — will require access to print-on-paper texts. Still others
maintain that computers are only tools, and while no one should oppose
the use of better tools, their uncritical worship is hard to justify. Useful
as the toilet bowl may be, it has no place in one's dining room. Even in
the corporate business world, where emphasis on "information
technology" has been the strongest, there is now a growing tendency to
question the technology's capacity to enhance profitability.

However, perhaps the strongest criticism of the "information
technology" assumption concerns predictions made about the future of
libraries. Technology is not an independent variable; its development is
highly sensitive to the economic, institutional and cultural contexts
within which it is located.   The assumption that the future of
technological evolution is both inevitable and predictable, based upon a
straight-line projection of current technological changes, is a highly
questionable one. Such predictions abounded in the late 1960s and 1970s,
and proved, for the most part, to be either highly exaggerated or
completely wrong. Predictions by Lancaster and others about books
becoming obsolete in twenty years, predictions made some three decades
ago, are but one example of skewed technological vision. In short,
straight-line extrapolations from recent technological trends that provide
no time frame are more in the nature of science fiction than serious
foundations for policy decisions for librarians. And especially when
dealing with the careers of LIS students, there is a responsibility to make
such predictions as carefully as possible. If one must make predictions,
one should at least specify a time frame: ten to twenty years for an
entering library professional, or the length of an average worklife of LIS
graduates?

Among the many critics of "information technology" in general, and of the Internet in particular, the work of Clifford Stoll is especially significant, coming as it does from one of the early pioneers of Internet. In his recent book (Stoll, 1995), Stoll argues that the Internet medium has been oversold. He maintains that computer networks encourage passive instead of active participation from users, thereby working against creativity and literacy, and undercutting the efforts of both schools and libraries. According to Stoll, this technology produces "mediocre writing" and "poorly thought-out arguments" because, without careful editing, one simply has no way of determining what is worth reading and what is not. In addition, Stoll points out that it is almost impossible to retrieve a message that was posted some time ago, making the whole Internet world a one-dimensional time experience that supplies only random current data, most of which is unchecked and unfiltered. And while Project Gutenberg has plans to scan in, at most, ten thousand books by 2010, this number sharply contrasts with the forty thousand books currently being published annually.

Assumptions Regarding the Needs of Library Users, the Functions of Libraries, and the Role of Librarians

According to the tenets of the Information paradigm, library users, be they businessmen, researchers, technicians, administrators or members of the public, employ libraries primarily for the purpose of obtaining "information." The need for "information," as a rule, is treated as being homogenous, irrespective of the type of users, the intensity of their need, the level of detail or comprehensiveness they require, or the complexity of their queries. The problem with this construction of users" needs is that it does not distinguish among different types of users.

Libraries of all types — special libraries as well as public, school, and undergraduate college ones — are likewise treated as being essentially identical in their function; they are all defined as providers of "information." Some special libraries are indeed charged with providing individuals engaged in scientific, administrative, and technical work with answers to their queries on demand. Preoccupation with rapidly informing a circumscribed group of clients, rather than with offering educational and cultural services to the public, is what differentiates their work from that of the vast majority of libraries, and determines the types of technologies upon which they depend. Given the above requirements, professionals who serve in such organizations need a strong subject

background even more than a general theoretical knowledge of the
formal rules of classification, abstracting and indexing. They have to
become specialists rather than generalists. Their task is to extract from
the vast amount of possibly informative texts those that will probably
answer their clients' inquiries. Such work requires familiarity with the
literature of their particular field, and necessitates that they acquire
appropriate textual materials for their libraries. Today professionals
working in such organizations must also be computer-literate,
knowledgeable about the construction and manipulation of databases, and
familiar with the process of searching databases. It is such skills that
differentiate them qualitatively from the vast majority of librarians, and
justifies their designation as "information managers." Despite the many
differences that exist among special librarians, their work is different
from that of most other librarians, with the exception of some individuals
who work in larger research and government libraries. They are also
different because of their commitment to serve a narrow and more
defined class of users, and to provide their clients with texts retrieved
with the help of computer-based operations. Generalizations that may
apply to them do not necessarily apply to any other librarians.

The artificial identification of all types of libraries with special
libraries has enabled adherents of the Information paradigm to claim that
these distinct types of work are one and the same. Despite the numerous
variations that exist among general libraries — a small one-room rural
library as contrasted to such institutions as the Chicago Public Library—
as of today their main function is to serve a mass public by providing
desired print-on-paper texts that are selected, collected, organized for
ease of retrieval, and then lent out. Unglamorous as it may appear,
public libraries are, and have always been, primarily about providing
reading material (i.e., texts in whatever format), to those who cannot
afford to own the thousands of books they will read over a lifetime. Their
other services — reference teaching how to use the library, how to choose
books, and how to find what material one needs to consult, are primarily
carried out by public, school, academic, and most special libraries in
order to support their principal function. Together, they form the
overwhelming majority of all libraries in North America.

The role has been judged as being a vital one by millions of U.S.
taxpayers who have repeatedly voted in favor of local bond issues to
support public libraries in their communities. They have done so because
they perceive libraries to be contributing to popular education, to the
raising of the level of popular culture and informed political

participation. Libraries have long been perceived as the great equalizers in American society — the Peoples' Universities.

As was already stated, most libraries dispense knowledge, ideas, aesthetic and inspirational materials, music, data, facts, potentially informative texts, as well as graphic illustrations, in computer and audio/visual formats. Such services are of special importance to young people, to the underprivileged, to immigrants, and to seniors who wish to read for personal improvement or entertainment rather than to obtain some isolated datum. Public librarians support individual adult learning activities that are today blanketing the North American landscape. Undergraduate libraries, especially, provide a vast store of textbook and nontextbook literature that would otherwise be unaffordable to most undergraduate students. In addition, school, public and undergraduate academic libraries also acquire selected portions of the graphic record that they integrate with courses taught at local educational institutions, by compiling lists of available texts on selected topics that may be eventually required by users. Public librarians provide services designed to help individuals select a sequence of texts to satisfy a particular interest. For those individuals who seek access to morally or politically inspirational reading, libraries act as repositories of general philosophical, literary, religious, and other needed "uplifting" material. Libraries also offer their users a vast range of additional services, such as reference, readers' advice, interlibrary lending, photocopying, access to the Internet and instruction in its use, as well as other technologies such as interactive CD-ROM products.

The functions of librarians are defined by adherents of the Information paradigm as being essentially that of "information" providers to their clients. All their other functions are treated as leftovers from the past, or simply ignored. Skills needed to operate libraries are perceived as being best modeled on those required by "hightech" special librarians, on the premise that the selection, acquisition, organization, storage, and retrieval of any "information" involves similar abilities, and when acquired, these skills would enable librarians to perform any type of "information" function and to become "professional information managers."

The proposition that the principal task of librarians is to provide "information" to clients is a logical extrapolation from the definition of libraries as "information" retrieval centers. This conception is questionable because it reduces the many functions performed by different types of librarians to one undifferentiated "information management" function. For most librarians, the work involved in informing their clientele is but a small part of their total everyday activity. Librarians perform many other professional-level functions that can not possibly be classified as "information" activities. The proposition likewise ignores the fact that there are vast differences in skills required by a Young Adult readers' advisor and an information analyst, occupations that have almost nothing in common except for a tenuous verbal linkage. In addition, one should keep in mind that the overwhelming percentage of librarians whose work requires them to inform their clients on matters of interest, do so primarily about bibliographic matters.

Underlying the contention that only the computer technology functions of libraries are of any permanent significance is the belief that the utility of print-on-paper books is on the decline, due to the fact that "information" can be more efficiently stored and retrieved by computers. Such an assumption is questionable. After all, besides being informative, books are also read for inspirational purposes (the Bible or Koran); for escapist reasons (a fast-moving "who-done-it"); for educational purposes (a nonfiction popular history), or for career reasons (a book on elementary accounting). On the other hand, there are a growing number of instances where computer-stored texts are far more efficient than the print-on-paper format. For example, chemical molecular structures, statistical data, and a large number of ephemeral materials are far better stored on-line rather than in hard copy.

More than half of the public library collections in the United States consist of fiction, and one-half to two-thirds of the books borrowed from libraries are works of fiction. The figures suggest the possibility that people use books for recreation and learning, as well as for general cultural awareness, quite as much as for "information." For example, during the period from 1990 to 1992 in the United States, printed fiction books were by far the largest category (5,764 in 1990 and 5,424 in 1991, as compared to 514 and 523 in agriculture, 2742 and 2,695 for science, and 2092 and 2421 for technology) (*American Library Directory 1994-1995*: 443-446).

Another error that is engendered by the close identification of libraries and books with "information" is the undervaluation of the importance of reading, an activity promoted by libraries. The act of reading a text is mind-altering, as well as qualitatively different from receiving discrete bits of "information." Reading involves an active interaction between the reader and the content of a text, together with logical analysis and emotional evaluation. In short, reading engenders a person's active participation, rather than a passive acceptance of messages. The reading of great literature provides not only pleasure and recreation, but also helps people acquire those basic elements of historical and social knowledge without which a full sense of community cannot develop. Such reading provides people with common myths, common ways of remembering their past, common objects of mirth, and the realization that their personal experiences of love, pain, anger, and hope are universal and come in a variety of forms. In short, reading of serious fiction provides material that is necessary to deepen self-awareness and individuality, at the same time that it opens the gates to a nation's common culture. Since few in North America can afford to individually own a large enough stock of such books, libraries are the sine qua non of wide reading and act as unifiers of a culture that is based upon something other than commercialized television and other types of mass entertainment. One of the principal functions of school and public library professionals is to foster such reading by their publics. The role is based on the awareness that a given society can survive only if it possesses enough "cultural glue" to hold it together. That "glue" is the culture's common cultural inheritance and particular values. As the community's gateway to knowledge, the library provides a basic resource for lifelong learning, for independent decision-making, and for cultural development.

Formal educational institutions are not the only agencies capable of providing the required socialization in our society. The learning experience of children in schools can be replicated for unschooled adults in other community organizations such as libraries. Through adult education, individuals become literate citizens and habitual readers. They also become far more employable. Activities of this type are quite different from what a conventional "professional information manager" is called upon to do.

Illiteracy is a major handicap for anyone living in a postindustrial society. Such individuals are massively disadvantaged in almost all respects, in employment as well as cultural and political affairs. Again, it is librarians who are called upon to play a major role in helping teachers and literacy volunteers to combat this debilitating condition. Crawford and Gorman are correct when they write that

> the true course is for libraries to be involved in adult literacy, to keep and expand children's book-reading programs; and to keep

on keeping on in the face of false nostalgia and furturistic blather. (1995: 126)

Libraries exercise a vital function in literacy education. They create public awareness of such campaigns and help with appropriate beginning reading texts and programs of daily readings of newspapers and fiction. By bringing literacy classes to libraries, teachers can accustom their students to using them, and thus continue reinforcing newly acquired reading skills. Libraries are also a major resource to independent learners.

Assumptions Regarding an "Information Industry" and "Information" Professionals/Managers

Over two decades ago Marc Uri Porat (1976) found that over half of the wages, and nearly half of the U.S. gross national product originated in "the production, processing, and distribution of information goods and services." Others have since maintained that "in the future, information professionals will be major leaders in the information economy." It has also been argued that because "information" is doubling every few years, there will be a growing need for "professional information managers." Much of the reasoning rests on such vaguely defined concepts as "information industry," "information society" and "information management."

The assumption made by supporters of the Information paradigm is that the "information profession" is an integrated category of essentially similar activities. The lists of fields that are supposedly part of this profession vary widely, depending on who compiled them, but include such categories as librarians - those who work in libraries; indexers — those who assign descriptors to documents; abstractors — those who write or edit brief summaries of the main points of the document; editors — individuals responsible for the style, content, consistency, and accuracy of publications; computer programmers/system analysts — those who write coded operating instructions and programs to direct computer operations; marketing/sales personnel — those who promote and sell "information technology" products and services; products development/planning personnel — individuals who formulate strategies for new products and services; and educational staff — those who instruct users and assist them in handling "information technology."

This and similar lists illustrate the fuzziness of the concept of "information manager." There is, after all, a profound difference between being a childrens' librarian and a systems analyst. Nor can any discussion of the concept be meaningful without a statement of the theoretical and practical commonalities shared by all subsets of "information management." Mere assertions of theoretical unity among such widely disparate industries as the development of computer-based information management systems for General Motors, and operation of a one-room public library in a small town, are not sufficient. Nor do they preclude the alternative interpretation of "information" work as consisting of a large number of activities that are related to each other only by the misuse of the term.

Lacking a reasonable definition of what an "information profession" is, one is forced to turn to such lists as the one compiled by the U.S. Department of Commerce and cited by Porat (1976). This list includes over one hundred occupations where "the major product is information." It is sufficient to mention only a few of the occupations that are listed in it — archivists, school library media specialists, information resource managers, information system designers, records managers, system analysts, and telecommunications network designers — to show the ambiguity of the "information profession" category. It is therefore quite reasonable to ask if there is really an "information profession" or if the label is an artificial construct, a reification, based upon philosophical notions about the nature of "information," rather than upon any empirical analysis of the actual attributes of certain occupations.

One final objection to any attempt to "converge" the library profession with "information management" is that only a very small proportion of such positions involve work that requires an in-depth understanding of information science theory, or a solid knowledge of computer technology. Most special librarians spend their workdays in much the same activities as other librarians, and therefore can not serve as a model for the "information manager" occupation. Surely it is illegitimate to include all special librarians in the category, not to speak of ALL librarians, just because of the minority of systems and other "high-technology" individuals.

In conclusion, the conflation of librarianship with "information management" has two unfortunate consequences: the creation of an impression that most of what librarians do, can be subsumed under "information handling" (such as educational, recreational or conservational work) should either be ignored, or marginalized into a subsidiary role, and secondly that the MLIS degree holders can handle, with competence, the whole gamut of "information-related" functions required by postindustrial society. Thus, on the one hand, the capability of the MLIS degree holders to carry on with the various types of "information" work is overstated; and on the other, an erroneous description is given of what most librarians actually do, and what skills they actually require on their jobs.

Assumptions Regarding Convergence in LIS Education

> Strategic planners in higher ed. are "deleting" programs that look embarassingly like trade schools, those that focus on technique have no theory base, and no theory-based research agenda... Stay with "library schools" if you like, but consider the long-range implications. (Pemberton, 1994)

Of all the "professional information management" occupations, only very few require the type of theoretical and practical preparation that is provided by the curricula of most LIS schools in North America or the United Kingdom. Most such occupations require a different set of skills, taught in different academic programs. Indeed, no one year-long LIS curriculum could possibly cover instruction in such diverse "information" activities as childrens" storytelling, searching on-line, conducting participant observation research, analyzing current political news, writing manufacturers" specifications, and providing competent referral interviews at crisis management centers. While courses in computer literacy and database construction have been introduced into the curricula of LIS schools, such extension of traditional library school offerings cannot justify the claim that their graduates will have the theoretical background or the skills required by an "emerging information market."

According to many advocates of the Information paradigm, traditional MLIS education is inadequate. What they are asking from LIS schools is a curriculum focused upon the requirements of the "information management profession." Their further contention is that current MLIS education, whose function is to prepare students primarily for positions within libraries, is incapable of accomplishing this, because most curricula do not focus sufficiently upon the management of "information." The advocates of convergence of library and "information management" courses in LIS schools generally agree that education for "information management" should take place within existing LIS schools rather than within computer or MBA/MIS programs. They further claim that only LIS-based programs can provide their students with both the necessary technical knowledge, (such as classification, database construction, and on-line searching), and a strong service orientation. Computer science programs are supposedly inadequate to the task because they are too focused on technology and systems; the MBA/MIS programs are inadequate because they are narrowly oriented toward company profitability, and upon internal company data.

Convergence theorists also seem to believe that such a curriculum could be fit into the time-frame of existing LIS programs. These assumptions are, once again, based on the central premise of the Information paradigm to the effect that librarianship is but a subset of the "information profession" and that, driven by "information technology," all the subsets are rapidly converging toward a single discipline based on the same body of theory and the same "information technology."

Until the expansion of business, scientific, and technical information centers and libraries in the 1960s, there was little pressure on library educators to establish separate programs to train "information managers." Only after computer-based technology made the construction and manipulation of massive databases possible was pressure exerted to provide such educational programs. In response to such pressure, a few separate "information studies" programs were started (e.g., Syracuse), but in the majority of cases the path taken was that of attempting to transform existing LIS library-oriented curricula into education for "information management." Proponents justified the alternative on the grounds that librarianship, along with all other "information" activities, is a subset of the "information profession," is converging with all the other subsets, and is being included within one general "information profession" curriculum (Galvin, 1995).

Arguments for convergence of LIS curricula into an "information management" program disregard the fact that the library profession encompasses many areas that are not directly derived from "information science" or based upon "information technology." Such subjects as adult education, literacy training, conservation and preservation of texts, analysis of rare book imprints, selection of texts for the social, political, and cultural needs of the reading public, and bibliographic instruction, while they may utilize computer technology, are no more dependent upon computer technology than they are on the printing press, the internal combustion engine, or the telephone.

Another question raised by convergence theory is whether it is really possible to add a whole series of additional "information" courses to the already all-too-short (in the United States under forty credit hours program) and overcrowded LIS curriculum, one of barely adequate length for a master's program in the basics of librarianship (Sineath, 1995). Clearly any large-scale infusion of additional "information" courses will result in a de facto substitution of "information" instruction for courses essential to library professionals, and will end up with the likely elimination of instruction in such subjects as Young Adult literature and collection management. In such a case, LIS school graduates will be inadequately prepared for professional library employment. Instead, they will find themselves in possession of a good deal of "information science" material that most of them will never need on their jobs. If, however, the proposed changes are to be implemented by establishing different "streams" within a unified LIS school program of "information studies," then the new curriculum will be nothing more than a form of divergence cloaked under the claim of convergence. Any master's degree curriculum, and especially one as short in duration as that of most U.S. LIS schools, would be far too superficial to serve as preparation for professional work.

Convergence theory rests on the highly abstract term "information," which leads to the clustering of different types of work activities, a flaw that is exacerbated by the refusal of the theory's supporters to provide a clear definition of what activities actually constitute the "information profession." Listing a few examples, as Pemberton does, such as "library science, records management, archives management, information science." (Pemberton and Nugent, 1995: 128), is not enough.

Two other reasons are cited for including "information management" studies within existing library schools. The first is that only in LIS schools will a proper service orientation be taught, and the second is that classification, which is a keystone activity of database construction, is the specialty of librarians. Both of these claims are hard to substantiate. There really is no logical reason why departments of computer science, or MBA/MIS schools, could not include a service orientation in their programs, teaching their students that a satisfied customer is a good customer. And, in the second place, classification is as old as Aristotle, Francis Bacon, Linnaeus, and Charles Darwin, and is most certainly not the exclusive "turf" of any one discipline, not even library/information science.

Indeed, a careful perusal of recent library literature strongly suggests that the proposed transformation of LIS education from one oriented to library service to one that is focused on "information management," is primarily motivated by political rather than intellectual considerations, as has been openly stated in recent library literature. For instance, we find an explanation of why the LIS school at Queens University in Northern Ireland transformed itself into a school of "information management":

> There was also the question of survival. It is extremely unlikely that Information Studies would have been allowed to continue with its postgraduate diploma course in librarianship, given the high unit costs of provision, the falling demand for places and the continued depressed state of the employment market. (Martin, 1991: 27)

Such considerations may well have been what Galvin had in mind when he wrote that

> as traditional public sector library job markets have dried up, schools of librarianship have been struggling, with varying degrees of success, to convert themselves from single product industries into multipurpose schools of the information professions. (Galvin, 1995: 8)

It is difficult to escape the conclusion that the attraction of convergence theory for many LIS faculty is based upon more than purely academic considerations. The following institutional and political factors seem to play a role in the tropism towards education for "information management."

- It provides an appearance of a unified theoretical underpinning that librarianship does not possess, but which is required for survival in the currently shrinking academic environment.
- It helps to give substance to the claim that graduates of these programs possess skills that have a far wider application than work in institutional libraries, a claim which is especially important in an environment when almost all libraries are reducing their staffs, while LIS schools are overproducing graduates for a shrinking market.
- Convergence theory helps reinforce the promise of LIS schools that there is a growing demand for "information managers" in an

"information society."
- It suggests greater access (than would a degree in librarianship), to new electronic technologies that are coming on-stream in business or industrial "hightech" libraries.

In conclusion, the assumptions of convergence theory about needed changes to LIS curricula appear aimed at a reinterpretation of the basic goal of library education to provide well prepared professional librarians for the library employment market. Instead, the convergence theorists' goal appears to be to provide an education that will be almost exclusively focused upon the creation of a corps of "information managers," a change that is certain to cause great harm to the library profession. To help visualize this unfortunate result, one needs only to ask the following question: if LIS schools were to decide to follow the advice of the convergence theorists, who would continue to provide training for the thousands of future public, school, and undergraduate academic librarians? As John Berry recently wrote, "Librarians must support those programs that offer education for future LIBRARY leaders" (Berry, 1995: 6).

In the business world, no manufacturing corporation with a well-established demand for its product would dream of reorienting its line without first commissioning a market survey to determine the potential demand for the new product that is to replace the existing one. Why then are LIS schools considering doing so without first conducting a study of existing job opportunities for their "information professionals" in nonlibrary "emerging information markets"?

Assumptions Regarding Employment in the "Emerging Information Market"

Placing a wide variety of disparate occupations under an "information sector" serves to gloss over major differences between them. Their connections, if any, need to be demonstrated rather than assumed. Such global schemes do not explain why it is useful to group lawyers, real estate appraisers, librarians and photographers into one single occupation: "information worker." Unlike other sections of this critique, the availability of a nonlibrary "emerging information market" to MLIS degree holders can best be assessed through empirical research rather than through an analysis of current library literature. However, before presenting the author's research results in this area, it was necessary to unravel the web of semantic confusion caused by a vague vocabulary. One aspect of the confusion is the claim that there is occurring an expansion of an "emerging information employment market." The claim is based on the contention that the "information industry" sector of the economy already accounts for a major share of the Gross Domestic Product, and continues to grow. Indeed, the claim is made that more than half of the U.S. workforce is in the "information" sector of the economy.

Supporters of the Information paradigm further argue that in order to cope with the flood of "information" being produced, more and more skilled "information managers" are needed. Businesses, they claim,

are increasingly depending on information and its technology to survive and succeed in the turbulent environment of the 1990s . . . information and its technologies are vital organizational resources. (Laribee, 1992: 17)

A further claim is that the "information explosion" will continue to grow as technology evolves, and as the importance of "information systems" continues to increase, creating an ever larger market for "professional information managers," many of whom will be MLIS degree holders.

The whole notion of a rapidly expanding "information industry," which purportedly will constitute a major new market for LIS school graduates, rests, as noted earlier, on the uncertain definition of what constitutes the industry. The wide discrepancy of answers to the question — from over one hundred separate activities listed by Porat, to more limited lists provided by others — is proof that there exists no agreement on a definition of the industry. It also suggests that the whole notion of an integrated "information industry" may well be more of a rhetorical device than an empirically verifiable fact. As for the viability of the "Information Brokering" alternative for any substantial number of MLIS degree holders, almost all accounts in current LIS literature agree that this work is not economically viable. Most individuals who have tried to make a living as "information brokers" discovered that it takes far too much time to obtain contracts.

In addition, there is much ambiguity in the contention that librarians are "information professionals." As we have already seen, the beginnings of a distinction between general librarians and "information managers" occurred some decades ago, as a reflection of the growing distinction between special librarians who were providing scientists, government officials, and businesses with factual and bibliographic data, and general librarians who provided a wide range of services to a diffused public. As the range of services provided by special librarians and information analysts expanded due to the impact of computer-based technology, the divergence grew, until today there remains little more than a verbal crossover between the two professions. Therefore, to confuse the two groups, either in their training or in their potential employment markets, is to distort reality. Such confusion becomes especially problematic when library school graduates begin to follow up on employment advertisements for positions like "Information Systems Manager" and discover that the skills they acquired in their LIS courses are not at all applicable to tasks involved in managing large-scale automated transfers of financial or geographic data. Nor will the gulf between these two professions appear any less significant when LIS school graduates attempt to join either the Canadian Information Processing Society or the National Federation of Abstracting and Information Services (United States), and discover that the members of these organizations are engaged in work that is totally different from that for which they had been trained.

The few empirical studies of the problem agree that today nonlibrary "information" employers are looking primarily for subject expertise plus administrative skills, electronic communication and computer ability, as well as aggressive business-oriented personalities, rather than for a hybrid of library/computer literacy gleanings. Given the fact that many of the emerging "information" positions in government or business organizations require primarily business or computer-trained individuals, MBA/MIS degrees are far more attractive to potential employers than degrees from LIS schools. This is borne out by the content of employer advertisements that call for skills slimly offered by the curricula of the MLIS programs. Indeed, MLIS-taught skills are not perceived by the majority of the "emerging market" employers as being really relevant to most jobs in their organizations. Also deserving of note is that hardly anyone outside the library profession, and far from all who are inside, gives such claims much credence.

What seems probable is that, instead of a single "information employment" market, there exist two distinct ones: the traditional general library market, which preferentially hires LIS graduates, and the new "hightech information market" that employs a very small minority of LIS school graduates. As John Berry has pointed out, an overwhelming majority of LIS students at Indiana University go into library work (115 out of 118 in 1993) (Berry, 1995: 6).

Richard Apostle and I first began to formulate our segmented market hypothesis after we conducted an extensive review of LIS literature on the subject. The literature seemed to indicate that "information management" jobs constituted a conglomerate of quite dissimilar occupations, only loosely gathered together under the umbrella "information" concept, and that the optimistic predictions of a growing demand for MLIS degree holders in that market could probably not be substantiated empirically. In order to examine this hypothesis, we asked for, and obtained, a grant from the Social Sciences and Research Council of Canada to conduct a series of labour market studies whose results are presented in chapters 5 and 6.

Are the Two Paradigms Reconcilable?

The Library Service and the Information paradigms have many areas of convergence.* Among these are the beliefs that

- librarianship is a unitary profession, with a distinct body of theory and specialized skills;
- librarianship requires special professional education (LIS) schools;
- library and information science are closely related;
- their commonality is based upon a single set of theoretical propositions as well as related functions;
- they have an intrinsic social value that warrants an enhancement of their professional status, greater prestige, and higher incomes;
- it is appropriate for LIS faculty, irrespective of their specializations, to belong to a single academic unit.

Their principal areas of disagreement are

---

*   For a clear statement of this, see Alliance of Libraries, Archives and Records Management (A.L.A.R.M.), *Towards a Strategy for Human Resource Development in Libraries, Archives and Records Management.*

- a tendency of the supporters of the Library Service paradigm to present a rather amorphous conception of its principal function, as against the focused definition of the Information paradigm;
- the divergence between the Library service paradigm's concern with cultural/educational services, and the emphasis of the Information paradigm's supporters on information retrieval in the sciences, technology, and administration;
- a difference in primary users, with the Library Service model concerned primarily with the general public, while the the Information paradigm concentrates upon the needs of a narrowly defined clientele of technical, scientific, and administrative personnel;
- a divergence of motivations, with the Library Service paradigm interested primarily in the "public good," whereas the Information paradigm seeks for the most part to enhance profit and service-for-pay;
- the Library Service paradigm's focus on the preservation, classification and circulation of print-on-paper texts, as against the emphasis of providing access to electronically stored data.
- a focus on reading for its own sake, as against concern with retrieval and utilization of informative materials;
- a basically reactive/advisory rather than proactive and prescriptive approach to professional service;
- a conception of the profession's mission as being basically for education, recreation, and cultural resource enhancement, as against service to business, science, and technology. The different attitude of the Library Service paradigm toward "information" technology — as being a very useful tool — contrasts with the Information paradigm's assertion that the technology is central to the profession.

Conclusion

The question posed by a review of the literature generated by the conflict between the Library Service and the Information paradigms is whether the conflict is, in fact, one over substance or illusion. Is it really warranted by any empirical findings, or is it built on a tangled web of theoretical postulates? Is it really necessary to take up one side as against the other in the struggle for the soul of a profession, or is the conflict more imaginary than real? Could it possibly be that a careful empirical investigation into the phenomena in question would reveal that librarianship is no longer a single, monolithic profession, but rather has become bifurcated into two quite distinct, though somewhat overlapping, ones? Are there now two separate professions, with each having a very distinct set of clients, distinct theoretical underpinnings, distinct skills, and distinct tools? Does the Information paradigm represent an attempt to fit all of the disparate activities of librarianship into one single model, that of the information centers and special libraries? Does its description of the work of most librarians correspond with empirical reality? The following empirical chapters were designed to explore these questions.

Notes

1. For an in-depth discussion of the two paradigms see Vakkari, 1994 and Miksa, 1992.

2. An information center is a government, association, or privately supported organization, usually mission-oriented, accomplishing in-depth acquisition, storage, retrieval, and analysis of significant information or data pertinent to the mission (Kochen and Donahue, 1976: 14). Such centers are established with a view of supplying an even more specific service, tailored to the needs of an elite clientele involved in advanced and often multidisciplinary research and development (Kochen and Donahue, 1976: 8).

3. The vocabulary of the Information paradigm has not as yet become consolidated; some individuals use the term "information professional," others talk about "information managers." In order to avoid confusion, I have combined these two designations into "professional Information manager."

4. "A library is a collection of graphic materials arranged for relatively easy use, cared for by an individual or individuals familiar with that arrangement, and accessible to at least a limited number of persons" (Harris, 1984: 3).

5. A typical example of such misuse of the term is the following newspaper quotation: "Economic Information has almost always been conveyed in a manner that people can't comprehend," said Gary Rabbior, president of a nonprofit organization. *(Halifax Chronicle Herald*, Wednesday, March 6, 1996, p. A5).

CHAPTER 2

THE IMPACT OF TECHNOLOGICAL CHANGE
ON THE WORK AND SKILL PATTERNS OF THE
LIBRARY PROFESSION IN CANADA

As the foregoing chapter suggests, there are a number of basic questions emerging from the conflict of paradigms that concern current work patterns in Canadian librarianship. We will begin an analysis by examining the extent to which the work settings, skills, and experiences of Canadian librarians have been transformed by new computer-based technologies. Given traditional North American attachments to notions about the inevitability of economic progress, and the central role of technology in economic improvement, it has been customary to make linear projections of technical trends we see about us into the indefinite future. More specifically, the Information paradigm suggests that "information" is the central component in the new postindustrial society, and its most dynamic source of employment. In terms of libraries as settings, this perspective leads to an expectation that libraries will move in the direction of having the same functions and purposes, with new library expansion being modeled on special libraries, or large research libraries that cater to scientists. Correspondingly, it can be inferred that the noninformation capacities of libraries, especially in public, school, and undergraduate university libraries, will be diminished.

The Information paradigm also leads us to anticipate that the skills needed to run libraries will be homogenized and will be modeled on the skills needed to run special or research libraries. Further, the acquisition, storage, organization, and retrieval of any kind of "information" involves essentially identical skills that individuals, once they have acquired them, can utilize in any sort of "information" work. Finally, it is assumed that one or two year postgraduate programs in library and information science will prepare individuals to perform any kind of information work competently. In particular, teaching computer literacy, and database and file construction skills to students in library and information schools will qualify them to act as "information managers." To address these questions, we conducted a national survey of Canadian librarians in the first half of 1994. We will present our basic findings, and then discuss their ramifications for the basic debate that informs our study.

Findings

At a descriptive level, the librarians and information scientists in Canada in our study, which was conducted between January and August 1994, tend to be overwhelmingly full-time employees. Only 5.4 percent of the sample of 555 were employed on a temporary basis and 7.1 percent were working part-time. In keeping with general employment patterns in the country, which are reflected in the sample framework (see Appendix A), 37.7 percent of the professionals in our study work in public libraries, 7.4 percent in schools, 29.4 percent in university or college libraries, and 25.5 percent in special libraries ("special libraries" include the National Library, CISTI, provincial libraries, and other government libraries, as well as public and corporate institutions people designated as "special").[1] It should also be noted that over half (56.3 percent) of the special libraries are located in Ontario. When one examines the specific areas in which people work, one finds, as indicated in table 1, that the three predominant departments, in terms of primary responsibility, are administration, one- or two-person libraries, and collection management and development. One and two person libraries, not surprisingly, tend to be concentrated amongst school and special libraries.

In terms of career tracks, a majority of the respondents indicated that they had worked in either acquisitions, circulation, or reference service for at least six months before entering a professional library program. Approximately one-quarter of the respondents had a second graduate degree in addition to an LIS degree. The most frequently reported additional degrees were masters of arts in the humanities, education, and the social sciences. Over 40 percent of individuals holding such degrees reported that their degrees are very important to their work; a disproportionately large number of them are employed in university or college libraries. The median income category for the entire sample is $40,000 to $49,000 per year. Individuals employed in school and university libraries were particularly likely to report incomes higher than these amounts.

Table 2 provides a detailed breakdown of how individuals in the study allocate their time in a typical week. As shown in this table, the major patterns reflect occupational responsibilities.

TABLE 1. DEPARTMENT IN WHICH INDIVIDUAL WORKS

Acquisition	9.4%
Administration	18.5
Adult/community services	7.2
Automation and systems	4.1
Archives	0.7
Cataloguing	7.9
Children/young adult	3.5
Circulation	1.3
Collection management/development	10.5
Media	0.6
Reference	14.6
Serials	0.4
User education	0.4
One/two-person library	15.0
Other	5.9

Administering and supervising, reference service, and collection development account for over half of the working time for the respondents. Collection development time is particularly important in public and university libraries. Reflecting the above occupational and work task requirements, we find that administration and supervisory skills are the most frequently reported competencies, with 36.7 percent of the sample reporting these skills as necessary for library work. Reference skills, at 22.6 percent, are the second most important. In terms of skills that people believe they will be needing to acquire or improve over the next five years, computer searching skills rate highest at 22.2 percent, but they are closely followed by administration and supervisory skills (21.2 percent) and automated systems skills (18.6 percent).

As indicated in table 2, work with computer systems is a widespread expectation, and 93.4 percent of the respondents report that they do some such work in their present jobs. The proportions of time spent working with computer systems are moderately high. Of the sample, 15.9 percent reported spending only 1 to 10 percent of their time during a typical month on such work. However, the proportions for 11 to 25 percent of time, 26 to 50 percent, and 51 to 75 percent, respectively, increase to 25.3 percent, 25.9 percent, and 20.5 percent. Public librarians were particularly likely to report doing "housekeeping tasks" (cataloguing, circulation, serials) while school librarians tended to focus on the retrieval of factual information. It is also significant to note that over half of the respondents state that the optimum level of training they need for computer work involves only on-the-job training. A further 19.9 percent indicate that vendor workshops sufficed and another 11.7 percent mentioned one- or two-week formal courses. In sum, over four-fifths of the sample respondents indicated that the maximum training required was two weeks or less.

Although new technology-related skills do not account for much work time on average, we can sharpen the differences among library types by examining the perceived importance of these skills. If one includes automated system management, bibliographic databases construction, computer programming, non-bibliographic database construction, and systems analysis and design from table 2 as important new skills, there is an interesting association between library type and the perception that any of these skills ranks among the three most important an individual possesses. As shown in table 3, there is a marked contrast between public, school, and academic libraries, on the one hand, and special libraries, on the other, in the number of people claiming new skills as important competencies. Among special libraries, 23.9 percent claim one or more new skills among their three most important, as contrasted with only 10.5 percent of public libraries.[2]

TABLE 2. PROPORTION OF WORKING TIME SPENT ON
TASKS IN A TYPICAL WEEK

Acquisition/ordering/purchasing	4.49%
Administering/supervising	22.94
Archives management	0.51
Automated systems management	3.29
Bibliographic database construction	0.92
Bibliographic instruction	2.66
Cataloguing	4.54
Circulation	2.83
Classification and indexing	2.55
Computer programming	0.36
Collection development	9.33
Computerized searching	6.21
Research	3.65
Media production	0.34
Nonbibliographic database construction	0.34
Preservation and conservation	0.46
Public programming	1.89
Reference service	19.63
Serving specialized audiences (e.g., shut-ins)	0.99
Working with specialization material (e.g., government documents)	2.27
Working in specialized subjects (e.g., Spanish poetry)	1.57
Systems analysis and design	1.12
Other, please specify _____	7.11

In terms of assessing the validity of the assumptions upon which the Information paradigm is based, if one adds the time that librarians spent on automated systems management, bibliographic database construction, computer programming, nonbibliographic database construction, and systems analysis and design, two striking facts emerge. The first, as shown in table 4, is the very small proportion of time that these five "cutting-edge" information management skills occupy in the time budget of Canadian librarians.

TABLE 3. LIBRARY TYPE BY MANAGEMENT INFORMATION SKILLS RANKED IN TOP THREE COMPETENCES

Library Type	New Skills			
	0	1	2/3	
Public	45.9%	43.6	10.5	(209)
School	46.4%	36.6	17.0	(41)
Academic	44.8%	36.8	18.4	(163)
Special	34.5%	41.6	23.9	(142)

The second is that there is a significant difference in the use pattern of these skills as between public, school, academic, and special libraries. The most vivid illustration of this is the difference indicated in the "pure-wool" information management activities — bibliographic and nonbibliographic database construction. Of the librarians in public settings, only 1.4 percent considered these types of database construction to be among the three most important ones for their work (see table 5). Among academic librarians, only 3.4 percent chose bibliographic and 0.8 percent nonbibliographic activity. In sharp contrast, among special librarians there were a combined 8.9 percent who so chose.

We received a considerable amount of qualitative information from our respondents that helps us to understand the specific nature of the work being done in Canadian libraries, and about the images librarians have of their work environments. In terms of skills, public librarians, as suggested above, now do much of their routine housekeeping via

TABLE 4. LIBRARY TYPE BY PROPORTION OF TIME SPENT
WORKING WITH MANAGEMENT INFORMATION
SKILLS (As Percentage of Typical Work Week)

Library Type	Automated Systems Management	Bibliographic Database Construction[3]	Computer Programming	Nonbibliographic Database Construction	Systems Analysis and Design
Public	3.66	0.23	0.33	0.21	0.86 (145)
School	4.33	3.22	0.56	0.18	0.64 (27)
Academic	2.35	0.63	0.33	0.62	1.13 (116)
Special	4.32	1.43	0.28	0.37	1.57 (100)
Total	3.48	0.87	0.33	0.37	1.10 (388)

various electronic systems. However, like school librarians, public librarians do answer a considerable number of user requests of bibliographic and statistical information using CD-ROMs.[4] The school librarians in our study, while they do focus on the retrieval of factual information, do get access to new services and public statistics through the use of CD-ROMs, Internet, and Schoolnet.

Academic librarians employ many of the same technical skills as school and public librarians, but they tend to spend more of their time showing students and staff how to find answers for themselves. One academic librarian facetiously asked, "Is coercing or cajoling faculty a skill?" Individuals employed in public, school, and academic libraries also tend to have a different orientation to their work with computers than do special librarians. They are more inclined to see the "human" side of the person-machine interaction. As one public librarian put it, "computers seem to need a lot of TLC, and downtime is a nightmare for public service." These individuals also tend to look at the utilization of

TABLE 5. LIBRARY TYPE BY PERCENTAGE OF RESPONDENTS
WHO CLAIM MANAGEMENT INFORMATION SKILLS
AMONG THREE MOST IMPORTANT WORK SKILLS

Library Type	Automated Systems Management	Bibliographic Database Construc--tion[3]	Computer Programming	Nonbibliographic Database Construction	Systems Analysis and Design
Public	20.7	1.4	2.1	0.0	5.5 (145)
School	20.0	0.0	0.0	0.0	3.3 (30)
Academic	16.9	3.4	0.8	0.8	5.1 (118)
Special	17.6	8.8	0.0	0.1	5.9 (102)

computer technology from the perspective of local users. One such individual was quite critical of vendors who want to sell packaged software, claiming that vendors are frequently "not advanced enough to understand the present realities of how people want to use their systems."

By contrast, individuals working in government or special libraries tend to indicate a wider and more complex range of technical skills. These may include everything from network administration to software installation and maintenance, hardware maintenance and training, as well as the use of electronic mail and CD-ROMs. Special librarians also emphasize the extent to which they are involved in demanding subject searches or actual research. Special librarians who work in the private sector emphasize client orientation, time constraints, and the absence of technological skills amongst their clients. Individuals in private sector special libraries also make note of the extent to which their work involves "bottom-line consciousness" and self-select people who can work autonomously. As one respondent commented, "We have more "front-line" interaction, more cost accountability, more organizational vulnerability, and a heavy emphasis on public relations which is for self-starters and independently motivated workers only." While the emphasis here is more on the technical aspects of work, there are irreducible interpersonal components to their work. As one person working in a legal library put it, "You don"t have to kick drunks out of the library. Instead, you must know how to calm down impatient lawyers nicely." Our sample also included questions about nonbibliographic work as well as other reasonably unconventional tasks. Over 65 percent of the sample indicated that non-bibliographic work requires 10 percent or less of their time. However, a fairly high proportion of the respondents reported doing some form of nonbibliographic information work where such work was defined as the "obtaining of information through original research, retrieval of specific facts through oral interviews, and handling the flow-through of materials on a production line." Over half of the public librarians reported providing some references about their community, as well as providing oral information concerning community activities. Special librarians reported that they were particularly likely to do surveys of current literature or conduct original research on some subject area, while school librarians reported that they obtain specific subject data quite frequently for their students. In terms of other nonconventional tasks, we found that university and special librarians frequently work with unpublished "grey" literature, while special librarians are particularly likely to have to deal with "in-house reports."

Over three-quarters of the respondents in our study stated that some of the technologies they work with could be described as "information technologies." Further, over half of these individuals acknowledged that some differences do exist between "libraries and information centers." However, only 29 percent of the respondents claim that they work in an information center and, not surprisingly, these individuals tend to be special librarians. Further, virtually all of the people who say they are working in information centers view their work as differing from that in public, school, and academic libraries. Along the same lines, somewhat over half of our respondents also recognize differences between the terms "information professionals" and "librarians." One-hundred and fifty-one individuals claim that they work as "information professionals," while 156 assert that they are employed in information centers. When asked to what extent people think different kinds of libraries will be replaced by electronic data banks over the next ten years, academic, and particularly special, libraries were singled out as ones in which this would happen "a lot." Over 54 percent of the respondents thought this would happen to special libraries and 31 percent to academic libraries, as opposed to 12 percent for school libraries and 10 percent for public libraries.

Almost 72 percent of our respondents are women. There are few gender differences of note in our national sample. Women are somewhat more likely to work in public libraries and less likely to be employed in academic libraries. Women are less likely than men to be employed as administrators (although they do as much administrative work), and they earn somewhat less income for their efforts. Further, men are more likely to possess postgraduate degrees other than an MLIS. In terms of work time spent, men are significantly more likely to do automated systems management, cataloguing, and systems analysis, while women are more involved with on-line searching and public programming. Interestingly, women are more likely to think that considerable change is probable in different library systems. Women are more likely than men to see "some" or "a lot" of change coming, especially in school and academic libraries.

While Canadian librarians share many similar perceptions about changes that are likely to take place over the next decade, they have quite different interpretations of these changes. Public, school, and academic librarians jointly share the perception that new communication technologies will be integrated into existing library facilities, rather than displacing them. As one public librarian puts it, ""I see our library system growing, as our population grows; becoming more cost-effective; net-working with other libraries more; using new forms of communications and information technology; training staff more thoroughly; focusing more on providing information while still providing material strictly for recreation." There is a common expectation that public, school, and academic libraries will retain a multiplicity of functions. Public libraries will continue to be community centers and sources of recreational reading, Teacher-librarians will continue to be involved in the educational process, and academic libraries will retain their custodial functions. As one school librarian suggests, "teacher-librarians teach students how to learn by finding information and using information, but they also help to develop a love of reading and an understanding of our literary heritage." There is also a shared assumption that libraries as physical entities will remain in place. One academic librarian states, "a librarian by definition seems to be linked to a place which houses books, etc. The information profession is not dependent on one place; information is found wherever it is available."

Many respondents have doubts about the concept of an "information professional." One public librarian states that "an information professional is a librarian without the degree or formal training." There is some skepticism amongst these librarians about the concept of information centers as opposed to libraries. One academic librarian suggests that the concept information center is a "buzz word," and states that "our library was originally called a Learning Resources Center (for twenty-five years), but we had to constantly explain that Learning Resources Center meant library, so we changed to "library."" Still, most individuals distinguish information centers from libraries in a consistent fashion. As one public librarian puts it, "An information center implies multimedia and less emphasis on printed materials; the term also implies emphasis on referral services and less emphasis on collections." Extending this thought, another public librarian states, "A librarian is or should be open to all kinds and formats of information, including nonprinted ones, whereas information professionals are more oriented to given formats. This points out a further significant difference, namely, a librarian mediates both the patron and the file, whereas an information professional acts as a conduit to the file." Some public librarians also raised the prospect that the coming changes in librarianship may create greater polarization between those who can afford to buy information and those who can not. "There will be no free ride on the information super highway unless there is a radical change in international social structures, which will be most unlikely." There is also some concern that the new technology will lead to the presence of more machines and fewer staff in traditional libraries.

In addition to the primary lines of interpretation that join public, school, and academic librarians, there are some persistent subthemes that are indicative of a desire to counter the status claims sometimes associated with the notions of "information center" and "information professional." In this subtext, information centers are described as more restricted settings, with a narrower range of services. One public librarian described an "information centre" as "an area of the library which is designed to answer quick reference questions, not any that require research," while an academic librarian dismisses the term as "a meaningless phrase," "it's the booth at the Bay that tells you what floor luggage is on." By contrast, libraries are regarded as settings that utilize a wider range of media to provide a wider range of services. As one public librarian puts it,

> The provision of information is only one segment of the service
> of a library. A library exists to provide access to the experience

of reading—to the ideas, thoughts, joys, and cultural insights contained within the world's libraries. When the typical library user comes in to locate the *Odyssey* or the *Edible Woman* or the *Tempest* or *Gerald's Game* (or *Madonna's Sex!*), it is not information that they are seeking.

In a parallel fashion, questions are raised about occupational concepts. "An information professional does not need an MLIS — they could be a clerk, a library technician, or a computer specialist, and they may perform a more focused duty, as opposed to the broad range handled by librarians." Another public librarian goes further, dismissing information professionals as "the technician, the "CD surfer," the "on-line roamer"." In a similar fashion, a school librarian comments,

> The connotation of "information professional" is that the "professional" delivers "information," an impersonal channel rather than a living medium. Better to be an intellectual "madame" than a "technopimp," useful though technology is.

By contrast, employees in special libraries, whether in government or the private sector, see more clear-cut differences between information professionals and information centers, on the one hand, and librarians and libraries, on the other. For example, one special librarian in the study suggested that "information centers seem to evolve around serving a special clientele, and they become more specialized and aware of technology."[5] Special librarians, perhaps extending a perspective built out of their own experiences, see a more complex and sophisticated technological future for librarianship. One individual commented that they anticipate

> total integration of library records and electronic links with other libraries, instant transfer of data, searching, locating, and retrieval from electronic sources as CD-ROMs and electronic document delivery.

Whatever the truth of these projections, respondents are quite sensitive to the current impact that labels and images have. One specialist librarian in the private sector reports that "in fact, our name changed last year from 'library' to 'corporate information centre,' mainly to try and reflect our changed role to our clients." Another such librarian reports that

> the term "information professional" has been co-opted, to some extent by computer scientists. In my own organization, a distinction is made between the branch having this technical expertise (Informatics) and that having the subject and information organization expertise (Library), with the result that the Library is "database administration" and Informatics controls and administers the LAN.

While their views do place an emphasis on transformations in contemporary libraries, special librarians also recognize the existence of a continuing role for "traditional" library systems.

> We shall always need quiet places for study and reflection. Libraries will retain their importance. Information is not self-organizing and librarians are the ones trained to organize it.

Some special librarians retain a commitment to an identity to a librarian. As one special librarian put it,

> Although the term librarian may be seen to be old-fashioned, the term information professional is both bland and nebulous. Calling ourselves professionals won't make people think we are professionals. I believe "librarian" is an honourable term.

The francophone respondents tend to divide along the institutional lines discussed above, with special librarians having views that differ systematically from those of public, school, and academic librarians. However, these differences are muted, lacking the ideological edge of the anglophone world. Our reading of the francophone qualitative responses suggests that the documentalist tradition that informs French academic and professional life in western Europe makes the debate between the library service and Information paradigms less salient to francophones. First, there is less disagreement about the implications of current technological changes for the organization and workings of libraries and information centers. One public librarian states,

Une bibliothéque contient des livres, revues, et journaux dans tous les domaines. Un centre de l'information contient des brochures, des rapports, des terminaux pour informer le plus rapidement possible. Il peut y avoir un centre de l"information dans une bibliothéque publique.

In a comparable fashion, a special librarian in the public sector comments,

La bibliothéque est davantage un endroit de "culture" où on acquiert, entrepose et prête de la documentation sous sa forme primaire (livres, périodiques, videos, disques). Elle peut aussi servir de lieu d'animation ou d'activities culturelles. Sa clientele est moins spécialisée que dans un centre de l'information. Un centre de l'information met l'accent davantage sur le traitement et le stockage de l'information factuelle et bibliographique.

The contrast between francophone librarians and information professionals overlaps in a similar way. One academic librarian says,

Le terme "bibliothécaire" fait plus référence à l'acquisition, à l'organisation, à la conservation et à la diffusion (contenant) de *documents*. Le professionnel de l'information est plus axé sur le *contenu* relatif du besoin exprimé par un client (emphasis theirs).

A special librarian in the private sector agreed, stating

1. Bibliothécaire répond à des demandes de: bibliographie, biographie, documentation, recherche en bibliothéque; 2. Professionel de l"information a à répondre à des demandes d'information, de l'actualité, et de comment utiliser les informations.

Conclusion

The findings from our national survey lend only modest support to the assumptions that come from the Information paradigm about library work and libraries as institutions. While there is a considerable amount of agreement across different library settings, Canadian librarians distinguish strongly among these various settings in terms of the probable changes that information technologies will bring, with special libraries remaining the focus of these changes. Further, when public, school, and academic librarians do anticipate technological change in their areas, it is predominantly with a view to improving the quality of existing services, especially in a period of economic constraint. Again, while there is a perception that all librarians will have to improve their ability to work with the new computer-based technologies, current effort devoted to such work is limited in many settings, and future skills are seen as requiring small amounts of time to learn them.

What emerges from the above analysis is a picture of Canadian librarianship in which the structure of library settings was distinctly bifurcated between public, school, and academic libraries on one side, and public and private special libraries on the other. These differences in settings are reflected in the work experiences of librarians in them, and are associated with the very different interpretations that Canadian librarians bring to the changing nature of their work. In other words, the Information paradigm is much more appropriate to experience in special libraries, and has limited applicability to the more traditional library world that is still organized around a library service ethic.

Notes

1. While our respondents reported that they are responsible for the supervision of other people, this supervision almost exclusively involves nonprofessional staff. The median number of nonprofessional staff supervised is 6.55 and these individuals tend, not surprisingly, to be located in public and university libraries. Almost 60 percent of the supervisors reported having no professional librarians working for them, with the median being only 1.45.

2. Interestingly, one public librarian listed "juggling" as another skill they possess. They suggest that with a shrinking budget, they have to "juggle" a town council, board, nonprofessional staff and community needs, as well as do grant applications.

3. This pattern is significant at the .001 level. None of the other arrays is statistically significant.

4. It should be noted that the school librarians in our study are a selected subset of school librarians in Canada because most of our

librarians possess formal professional credentials as librarians. As such, they tend to be more frequently located in large, urban high schools.

5.   One special librarian working in the private sector made an interesting distinction between libraries and information centers by proposing that libraries have "collections which are developed and maintained, while information centers may not have these 'on-the-spot collections" but concentrate on having information available "just-in-time.'"

CHAPTER 3

THE NATIONAL LIBRARY
AND THE CANADA INSTITUTE FOR
SCIENTIFIC AND TECHNICAL INFORMATION
(with Kim Adams)

As has already been stressed in chapter 1, the concept of "information" lies at the very heart of the paradigm that is currently challenging the traditional Library Service definition of librarianship. This chapter presents a comparative study of two major Canadian library organizations — the National Library of Canada (NLC) and the Canadian Institute for Scientific and Technical Information (CISTI). This study is based upon both an analysis of relevant literature dealing with the two organizations and a series of interviews conducted during the 1991-1993 period by the authors of this book. The study was carried out in order to determine the actual content of their work, and to evaluate the proposition that the function of libraries is to provide undifferentiated "information" to their users. We were particularly interested in finding out exactly how these organizations actually informed their publics. Do they provide exclusively bibliographic "information" — the usual activity of all libraries — or did they go beyond this traditional service and provide a spectrum of informative data and facts that went beyond bibliographic retrieval of textual and other graphic material potentially useful to their users?

In order to examine this question, we conducted a detailed historical study, as well as a series of interviews with staff members of the two organizations, on the assumption that the activities of the two major libraries of Canada — one with a scientific and technical content, the other with a humanistic one — would serve as indicators of whether or not libraries handle all types of "information," or only a narrow subset of informative material, that dealing with bibliographic matters. We proceeded first by considering the origins of these two organizations, evaluating/and the nature of their particular services, and paying special attention to any nonbibliographic activities that they many have offered. Our hypothesis was that neither the NLC nor CISTI offered much in the way of nonbibliographic services.

History

The seeds of a national library in Canada were planted many years before they reached fruition. Although John A. MacDonald spoke in 1883 of the urgent need to establish a national library (Dafoe, 1948: 15), the National Library Act did not come into effect until 1953. Before the establishment of the Canadian Bibliographic Centre, the National Archives had been carrying out many of the roles that national libraries perform in other nations, including collecting the national literature and composing a national bibliography (Lamb, 1970: 166). Copyright legislation required that a copy of all Canadian publications be deposited in the Library of Parliament. However, this library was not equipped to manage such a large volume of material and much of the collection remained uncatalogued (Gibson, 1948: 119). One of the first successful steps toward establishing a Canadian national library was taken in 1947 when the recently formed Canadian Library Association (CLA) united with a number of other learned societies to present a joint brief to the federal government regarding the functions and benefits of a national library (Donnelly, 1973: 73).

The particular appeal of this presentation was its suggestion that national library bibliographical service could begin without a new building or large collection, indeed prior to the establishment of the library itself. Parliament's positive response to this proposal soon led to the establishment of the Canadian Bibliographic Centre (Lamb, 1970: 166), which was set up in 1950 with a dual mandate: to compile a national union catalogue and a national bibliography (materials written by Canadians, or about Canada, or published in Canada) (National Library Advisory Committee, 1950: 199). In the case of a national bibliography, the Bibliographic Centre was to continue the work of the Toronto Public Library, which for nearly thirty years had produced *The Canadian Catalogue of Books Published in Canada, About Canada, as Well as Those Written By Canadians*. The centre began its work in a corner of the museum of the National Public Archives, and by 1951 it was operating out of its own office. It is important to underline the fact that this centre was considered as the essential first step to the establishment of the National Library, thereby clearly indicating the intended principal function of the NLC. The next major step in defining the prospective role of the NLC was the 1951 Massey Report. This report gave explicit recognition to the immediate need to acquire Canadian materials and to provide the space to accommodate them (Royal Commission on National Development in the Arts, Letters and Sciences, [Massey Report], 1951: 103-105). The mission of the future NLC was defined as that of providing informative bibliographic data and being the custodian of texts of Canadian origin and/or content, as well as providing an additional, nonbibliographic, function. The Massey Report noted that "it was generally assumed that a National Library would be a centre of advice and encouragement to local groups struggling with local library problems" (National Library Advisory Committee, 1952: 165-166; Canadian Library Association Bulletin, 1952: 6-7).

Unlike the United States, where the Library of Congress became a defacto national library, along with the National Library of Medicine and the National Agricultural Library, Canada established a national library that was separate from the parliamentary library. The National Library Act came into effect in 1953 and laid the foundation for the NLC's administration, funding, and mission. The NLC was linked administratively with the National Archives, and William Kaye Lamb, the Dominion Archivist, was appointed as Canada's first National Librarian. This fact delayed the separation of the NLC from the National Archives, which has yet to be fully accomplished. The act specified the "Powers and Duties" of the National Librarian, which included continuing the work of the Canadian Bibliographic Centre (producing a union catalogue and national bibliography) as well as building the NLC's collection and entering into exchange agreements with other domestic and international organizations (Donnelly, 1973: 97, 101, 115-116). Section 11 of the text laid out the deposit law that compelled publishers to deposit two copies of every book published in Canada with the NLC. Adequate facilities for a national library were not, however, to be realized for some time to come, although new facilities had been discussed since long before the founding legislation was passed. A new building, which provided sufficient room for staff and services, was only completed in Canada's centennial year, 1967.

As early as 1970 the space limitations of being housed together with the National Archives were recognized, and in his 1979 report, the new National Librarian, Guy Sylvestre, recommended the National Library building be expanded and the National Archives assigned a new home, a development that has yet to take place. The National Library's collection expanded over the years, especially with the move to new permanent quarters in 1967. In addition to gifts, associated with the centennial year, the growth of the NLC's collection has been based on purchased acquisitions and legal deposits (Kingston, 1988: 167). As the collection has grown, so too has the size of the library's staff. The NLC had 14 staff positions in 1953 when it was established, while recent figures indicate that now it employs 509 people (*Directory of Libraries in Canada*, 1994: 243).

With the retirement in 1968 of William Kaye Lamb, and the appointment of a new National Librarian, the post of Dominion Archivist was separated from that of National Librarian. The following year a further expansion of space and staff enabled the NLC to increase its acquisition program, as well as to begin production of a national bibliography and of a union catalogue. The possibilities offered by computerization played a major role in these activities. By the mid-1970s, implementation of automation was well under way, with the development of cataloguing standards. Modifications for Canadian requirements of the U.S.-developed Machine Readable Cataloguing (MARC) were accomplished, and the 1976 acquisition of an on-line library system (DOBIS) led to the automation of *Canadiana* and the *National Union Catalogue* (Kingston, 1988: 167).

While fulfilling its mandated function of conserving Canada-related texts and providing extensive bibliographic services, the NLC has been able to initiate and participate in a number of other activities. A Canadian Cataloguing-in-Publication (CIP) program for cataloguing materials prior to publication was introduced in 1976 (Kingston, 1988: 167). A Documentation Centre was created in 1970. It has since changed its name to the Library Development Centre, and provides documentation and advisory services to Canadian libraries. Important other services have been developed, such as the Music Division, the Multilingual Book Service, the Rare Book Division and the Canadian Book Exchange Centre, the Children's Literature Service, and the Library Service for Disabled Persons (National Library of Canada, 1987, 1988, and 1991; Kinston, 1988: 167). The NLC has also developed an international role. In 1975 it assumed the responsibility for managing the assignment of International Standard Book and Serial

Numbers (ISBN and ISSN) within Canada, and in 1976 it was asked to contribute data on Canadian Serials for the Conversion of Serials (CONSER) (Kingston, 1988: 167).

Canada Institute for Scientific and Technical Information (CISTI)

CISTI's history is quite different from that of the NLC. Its roots extend back prior to the establishment of the National Research Council (NRC), which is generally recognized as its parent institution. A de facto Canadian national science library existed long before it was officially recognized as such. The NRC's predecessor, the Honorary Advisory Council of Scientific and Industrial Research, was a group of nine volunteers established in 1916. Beatrice Walling became librarian and abstractor for the council in 1917 (CISTI News, 1984a: 2). Then, after the NRC was established in 1924, its chairman, Dr. Henry Tory, began to foster a library in order to provide national service to its scientific staff working in its research laboratories. In 1959, the National Librarian and the NRC president endorsed an informal agreement delimiting the collection and services of the NRC Library and those of the NLC. While the National Library was to focus on the humanities and social sciences, the NRC's library was to have the responsibility of a national science library, and to develop services designed to make its resources readily available to the Canadian scientific community. It was also to collect comprehensively in all fields of science and technology except medicine, zoology, botany, agriculture, geology, and mining engineering (Donnelly, 1973: 173). Additionally, all scientific and technical publications acquired by the NLC under depository regulations were to be left with the NRC Library.

Another seven years would elapse, however, before the national nature of NRC's library was given statutory recognition, when, after a revision of the NRC Act, the library was renamed the National Science Library (NSL). In 1966 it was given the additional function of being the National Bibliographic Centre for the Medical and Health Sciences. In order to meet this responsibility, the library began to hire staff members with a science and medical background, and to collect biomedical journals. It also published a list of these sources. In 1968 it established the Health Sciences Resource Centre (HSRC), and in 1970 it took responsibility for coordinating the American medical literature analysis and retrieval system (MEDLARS) in Canada (CISTI News, 1984a: 6).

The services of the NSL have grown over the years. One especially important development was the establishment of CAN/SDI (Canadian Selected Dissemination of Information). CAN/SDI is a computerized current awareness service that provides subject bibliographies of journal articles. After it became available nationally in 1969, the number of databases searched continued to expand in response to consumer demand. In 1972 the National Librarian, Guy Sylvestre, announced that the NLC was to become a CAN/SDI centre responsible for requests in the social sciences and humanities as well (Mauerhoff, 1974: 21).

Following the merger in 1972 of the NRC's Technical Information Services and the NSL, the Canada Institute for Scientific and Technical Information (CISTI), came into existence. Its predecessor; the NRC's Technical Information Services (TIS), had been created in 1945 for the purpose of assisting "small secondary manufacturing industries to keep up with the rapid advances in research and technology."

CISTI's birth was marked by the opening of a new building. At its opening, CISTI operated nine branch libraries for the NRC (Ontario Library Review, 1974). CAN/OLE (Canada Online Enquiry system), a service similar to DIALOG in concept, evolved from CAN/SDI. CAN/OLE was a pilot project that made its first appearance in 1974. Created to provide computerized access to scientific and technical literature, CAN/OLE provided access to four databases. In March 1976 an improved CAN/OLE was made available to the public (Bullock, VanBuskirk and Walshe, 1987: 133).

While the two national libraries have remained separate institutions, some consideration has been given to combining them. The 1979 NLC report recommended that responsibility for CISTI be transferred to the NLC from the NRC on the grounds that the general mandate of the NLC, as legislated by the National Library Act, included the science and technology functions performed by CISTI (Wees, 1979: ix, 45-55). As well, a 1969 cabinet decision directed "the National Research Council, under the general direction of the National Librarian, to develop in concert with existing information organizations, a national scientific and technical information system to encompass the natural sciences and engineering." The National Library's 1979 report discussed the insurmountable difficulties for the National Librarian in successfully directing such a process, given the structural and administrative autonomy of the two institutions (Sigert, 1992).

An issue of CISTI News honoring the organization's tenth anniversary (1984) described the need for a name change: "The NSL had indeed become a national agency for the storage, retrieval, and dissemination of the world's output of scientific literature, activities better described by the name Canada Institute for Scientific and Technical Information" (CISTI News, 1984b: 9). No moves toward amalgamation have occurred since that time.

Stated Missions and Overall Work of the Two Organizations

The National Library

Francis Donnelly's history of the NLC traced its role back to the Joint Brief presented to the federal government by the Canadian Library Association and other organizations. This brief had outlined the need to build a national literature collection, provide reference and information services, coordinate library resources, produce a national bibliography, promote Canadian authors and book designers, and supply technical services to libraries (Donnelly, 1973: 236).

There have been a number of subsequent reformulations. The 1979 report, *The Future of the National Library of Canada*, included four objectives for the National Library approved by the National Library Advisory Board:

(1) to gather, preserve, and make known the nation's literature and to provide national research, reference, and information facilities and services in Canadian Studies; (2) to locate and to facilitate bibliographical and physical access to the collections present in libraries across Canada; (3) to assure the coordination of and to advise on national planning for the provision of library and related services in Canada and to participate in international planning for library services; (4) to utilize National Library resources in the most beneficial and effective way to meet National Library objectives and goals, including representing the public need for information services to the Secretary of State and Treasury Board, and supporting initiatives that are clearly in line with the goals and objectives of the National Library. (National Library of Canada, 1979: 5)

In 1986, A *Study Team Report to the Task Force on Program Review* recommended the following objective for the NLC:

> To preserve and promote the literary heritage of the Canadian people and to facilitate the use of the library resources of the country by the people and the Government of Canada. (Task Force on Program Review, 1986: 122)

The National Library's 1991-1992 annual report listed three chief responsibilities for the library:

1. To collect, preserve and promote access to published heritage;
2. To foster library development across the country; and,
3. To encourage the sharing of resources among libraries. (The National Library of Canada, 1992b: 8)

The foregoing analysis suggests that the NLC offers primarily bibliographical services that are provided by most national libraries, such as reference, collections, interlibrary lending, and, in addition, only a small number of nonbibliographical programs. Although the parameters of these services are broad, they bear little resemblance to the services provided by a typical information analysis center or to nonbibliographic "information" work performed by a high-tech corporate library. However, the NLC does play a nonbibliographic coordination role on a national level and does negotiate exchange agreements with various institutions on a national and international basis.

As most general libraries, the NLC is organizationally structured according to the different services that it provides: acquisitions and bibliographic services, external relations, information technology services, and public services. These divisions are further subdivided into the acquisitions and bibliographic services (which include cataloguing and subject analysis, library standards, selection and acquisitions, Canadian theses, Canadiana, acquisitions and legal deposit, the Canadian Book Exchange Centre, and *Canadiana Editorial*). External relations consists of the Library Development Centre (LDC), publications and marketing services, and public programs and cultural events. Information technology services is made up of information analysis and standards, management services, systems and telecommunications support, user support, management services, systems maintenance and operations, and systems development. Finally, public services consists of reference and information services, music, rare books, reading room, union catalogue, interlibrary loan, multilingual biblioservice, children's literature, and literary manuscripts. As this enumeration of services suggests, the NLC has continued to emphasize its mandate to collect materials by and about Canada (in part through legal deposit) and to produce *Canadiana*, a bibliographic compilation. It also has maintained and developed collections and related services in a variety of specialized areas. In addition, books in languages other than English or French are circulated by its multilingual biblioservice to public libraries via regional deposit centres (National Library of Canada, 1989b: 23).

Apart from *Canadiana*, the NLC's publications range from the annual report and pamphlets publicizing various services such as interlibrary loan, to titles such as *Glenn Gould 1988*, the catalogue of the library's Glenn Gould exhibition. This exhibition is an example of one of the ways the NLC promotes the Canadian cultural heritage. It also stages and/or participates in a number of public programs and cultural events both as independent and cooperative ventures, an activity that, although customary for libraries, is not bibliographically related.

The NLC also carries out its library leadership role through national and international committee work, its involvement with the International Federation of Library Associations and Institutions (IFLAI), the development of library standards, as well as agreements that in part facilitate borrowing from other nations. One such project was the development of protocols — "well defined procedures and rules." Its Development Centre supports and seeks to further library development in Canada through its reference, referral, and liaison services, another nonbibliographic function. This center is used by the NLC's own staff, by a variety of Canadian and international librarians, and by members of the Canadian publishing and cultural communities (National Library of Canada, 1992a: 2).

In short, while the NLC is primarily concerned with providing such traditional bibliographically based library services as acquisitions, collections management, cataloguing and subject classification, reference, and interlibrary loan, it also plays a major role in professional library development in Canada, as well as in the development of national library service standards.

CISTI

Unlike the National Library Act, the National Research Council Act provided no specific direction for CISTI. The legislation simply stated that the NRC was to "establish, operate and maintain a national science library." CISTI's November 1990 Mission Statement (CISTI, 1990) read as follows:

The Canada Institute for Scientific and Technical Information is Canada's principal agent for the provision of comprehensive world-wide scientific, technical and medical information (STI). Its mission is to meet the STI needs of Canadians, including industry, universities, and governments. To achieve this mission CISTI will:

- develop and maintain an outstanding national resource of scientific, technical and medical information;
- develop, maintain, promote, and deliver quality information products and services in the fields of science, technology and medicine;
- develop expertise and knowledge for the creation, use, exploitation and advancement of world-class information products and services in the fields of science, technology, and medicine;
- provide STI services to support NRC's research and development programs.

The institution's 1992 strategic plan stated that its mission was to ensure Canadian access to the world's scientific, technical, medical, and related information (CISTI, 1992: 4). A quick guide to its services and products indicates that CISTI's services are divided up into reference services, database systems, current awareness services, document delivery services, publishing, and cataloguing products and services. Some of these services appear substantially different from those of the NLC — the current awareness service and the literature and "information" searches, including patent literature searches provided by the reference service (CISTI, 1994c: 8). As well, CISTI offers a service it calls "reference plus," which entails conducting literature and factographic searches and the sending of selected retrieved documents from its own collection to specific clients (CISTI News, 1994a: 1).

CISTI's collection is not restricted to Canadian scientific and technical materials. Between CISTI's main and branch libraries, the collection contains most of the world's significant scientific, technical and medical journals — some 54,000 serials titles in total — regardless of language or country of origin. It also possesses over half a million books and conference proceedings, more than two million technical reports in microform (CISTI News, 1994d: 7) translations of scientific articles and a registry of these translations (Sigert, 1992).

Nonbibliographic Work of Both Organizations

The National Library

As noted above, most of the National Library's work is very much in keeping with the traditional spheres of library work. However, there are certain activities that are nonbibliographical in nature. These primarily consist of the consultation services that are provided by the Library Documentation Centre. The NLC's work in creating databases is, for the most part, bibliographic in nature, as the databases are designed to provide computerized access to the textual and other graphic material contained in Canadian libraries. This function is virtually the same as publishing that material in print or microfiche form. The difference lies only in the format. Most of the NLC's computer-based work is likewise bibliographic or text-based, being intended to improve and speed up cataloguing and indexing, as well as the bibliographic retrieval process. Thus the function has remained the same, with the only change being the type of tools (computers) used.

The following brief descriptions and list of the databases currently maintained by the NLC were taken from the *Gale Directory of Databases* (Maraccacio, 1994):

1. Canadian Conspectus full-text, numeric bilingual database providing descriptions of the "scope, depth, and quality" of Canadian library collections. Canadian Association of Research Libraries (CARL) collect the data. Available online from Information Technology Services of the National Library of Canada.

2. Canadian Union Catalogue of Library Materials for the Print-Handicapped (CANUC:H): a bilingual bibliographic database of materials in braille, large print and talking books available for interlibrary loan from Canadian libraries and other organisations, it "includes a companion registry, Canadian Works in Progress (CANWIP), which lists prepublication titles produced by Canadian

nonprofit institutions serving visually impaired persons," and is available online as part of DOBIS Canadian Online Library System and as a private file, BLND, on BRS Online.

3.   DOBIS Canadian Online Library System. A bibliographic database which "Corresponds entirely or in part to the following 11 print, microfiche, or other online databases: Canadiana, Canadian Theses, CONSER Microfiche, LC MARC Fiche, Union List of Serials in the Social Sciences and Humanities (CANUC:S), Union List of Scientific Serials in Canadian Libraries (UNION), Canadian Locations of Journals index for MEDLINE, Cataloguing in Publication (CIP), Canadian Union Catalogue of Library Materials for the Print-Handicapped (CANUC:H), Canadian Works in Progress (CANWIP), and Union List of Canadian Newspapers (ULCN). Available online from Information Technology Services of the National Library of Canada.

4.   Union List of Serials in the Social Sciences and Humanities (CANUC:S) a bilingual bibliographic database listing social science and humanities serials in Canadian libraries.   Available in CD-ROM, microform and online as part of DOBIS Canadian Online Library System (Maracaccio, 1994: 138, 144, 263, 264, 839, 966, 1050). As this list reveals, the NLC's databases are automated union lists of materials available in Canadian libraries. Bibliographic and text-based, they are also available in non-electronic form, such as microfiche or hard copy. These sources, regardless of format, are in keeping with the mandate to create a national union catalogue. The construction of such a catalog, has from the very beginning, been considered as one of the primary bibliographic responsibilities of the NLC.

CISTI

The 1966-1967 Annual Report of the National Science Library characterized CISTI as "an information transferral agency" rather than a library in the conventional sense of the word (National Research Council, 1967: 23). Most of the work CISTI does is, however, library work in a traditional sense. As with the NLC, automation has been used at CISTI mainly for bibliographic purposes (computerized/on-line/automated directories and bibliographies) or extensions of those endeavours. A 1992 interview with a CISTI staff person indicated CISTI maintains and provides access to bibliographic databases: "We're not as big as DIALOG. CISTI has several services and, you know, interlibrary loans. Our aim is to provide access to the core files in science and technologies." CISTI operates a number of services that rely on the application of computer technology. Among these are database systems, current awareness services, document delivery services, and cataloguing products and services. Database systems, a service for researchers wanting to conduct independent on-line searches, consists of CAN/OLE (Canadian Online Enquiry Service), MEDLARS (Medical Literature Analysis and Retrieval System), and CAN/SND (Canadian Scientific Numeric Database Service). InfoAlert, MEDLARS, SDI, Table of Contents Service, and SwetScan make up CISTI's current awareness services, means by which people can be kept up-to-date on the topics of their choice. All of them are an extension of CISTI's Selected Dissemination of Information service. Document delivery services at CISTI include document searches and supply and translation searches. As well, CISTI's Service 2000+ provides ordered documents from the main collection so quickly they are guaranteed to be ready to be picked up by courier the next business day. CISTI also offers a variety of cataloguing products and services. ROMULUS, a CD-ROM product listing serials in Canadian libraries, was developed by both CISTI and the National Library of Canada (CISTI News, 1994c: 7). In addition, CISTI offers the on-line catalogue (on DOBIS) and union lists of serials available on-line with CAN/OLE and/or on microfiche.

The following databases are listed for CISTI in the *Gale Directory of Databases:*

1. CISTI Catalogue of Monographs (CISTIMON), bibliographic
2. CISTI Catalogue of Serials (CISTISER), bibliographic
3. Directory of Federally Supported Research in Canadian Universities (UNIVRES)
4. North American Translation Database, bibliographic
5. NRC Publications (NRCPUBS), bibliographic
6. Union List of Scientific Serials in Canadian Libraries (UNION), bibliographic

As can be seen, almost all of these databases are bibliographic in nature. According to the *Gale Directory of Databases* (Maraccacio, 1994), CISTI does, however, maintain two databases that are not strictly bibliographic, but rather numeric and properties — Metals Crystallographic Data File (CRYSTMET) and the Search Program for Infrared Spectra (SPIR) (Maraccacio, 1994: 175-1012). These databases contain raw scientific data made accessible by CISTI, but "none of the people that are involved in its operation have any library training at all. They are typically chemists who are nothing but chemists" (Sigert, 1992).

The 1992 strategic plan reveals CISTI's plans to move towards having more electronic sources: the overwhelming trend in the delivery of information, for reasons of speed, cost, and effectiveness, is the development of the electronic or "virtual" library. CISTI branches will move toward a "library without walls" concept, but to achieve this goal, the majority of STI (Scientific and Technical Information) will have to be available in electronic format, a high-capacity national electronic communications network will have to be in place, and interorganizational coordination to ensure trouble-free access to electronic files will be required (CISTI, 1992: ii).

An update to CISTI's strategic plan appeared in the June 1994 issue of *CISTI News,* including a mention of the development of the "virtual library" concept. According to this update, this concept would enable CISTI's branch libraries to offer a broader range of information resources. The CISTI branch at NRC's Institute of Biodiagnostics Research in Winnipeg is the prototype for this new-style library (CISTI, 1994: 4).

Conclusion

As can be inferred from the above material, some differences exist between the NLC and CISTI, with most of them having little or nothing to do with the actual function of these two institutions. The age of the two institutions is different. The NRC Library came into being in 1924, predating even the Canadian Bibliographic Centre (the NLC's predecessor) by nearly thirty years. As well, CISTI is a division of NRC, a crown corporation, whereas the NLC is equivalent to a government department in its own right. CISTI's budget is considerable higher, but its staff is considerably smaller (*Directory of Libraries in Canada,* 1994: 79-81, 243-45). CISTI's branches make it more decentralized and its work more dispersed geographically, while the NLC is operated almost exclusively out of Ottawa. CISTI's collections and services have a more specific subject focus than those of the NLC which has a rather general geographic focus. The NLC, has a broader subject focus, but its collection is primarily restricted to material by and about Canadians. CISTI has a more limited clientele to its services — scientists and business/industry people — whereas all Canadians have access to the NLC through their local libraries. CISTI actually has more direct contact with individual library users because its services are more directly accessed by individuals and companies; the NLC is more "a library's library."

The main difference affecting the work of these two organizations lies in their respective utilization of computer technology. Both make considerable use of automation, but their foci appear to be different. The CISTI databases are not all strictly bibliographic, whereas the NLC's are. Despite these divergencies, CISTI and the NLC have much in common; their similarities far outweigh their differences, and both are very much libraries, despite CISTI's claims to the contrary. They both provide interlending, automated access to their catalogued holdings on DOBIS, reference and referral, publications (both print and automated), and selected dissemination of information (SDI).

CHAPTER 4

THE CONVERGENCE OF
LIBRARY AND INFORMATION LITERATURE?
(with Paul Smith)

One of the assumptions of the Information paradigm is the proposition that convergence of the library and information sciences should lead to a growing overlap in the professional literature of the two fields. There are a number of different paths by which a "convergence" may occur, and they have different implications for our understanding of connections between the two fields. On the one hand, it is possible that an emerging set of commonalities motivates an increasing merger that may (or may not) become complete. Borgman and Schement (1990) label this a "paradigm shift." Alternatively, we may be observing a relatively modest overlap between two fields that maintain separate perspectives, but make occasional appearances in one another's literature. The empirical questions that flow from this contrast are (1) how much convergence or overlap has occurred? and (2) are there changes in this overlap or convergence over time?

Procedures

In order to examine the proposition that library and information science professional literatures are converging, we did a content analysis of fourteen representative English-language periodicals from the two fields for the period 1971-1991. We selected one Canadian library science journal (*Canadian Library Journal*), five U.S. library science journals (*Library Quarterly*, *Library Trends*, *Library Journal* [American], *Wilson Library Bulletin*, and *Library Resources and Technical Services*), and one British library science journal (*British*

Library Journal) to represent English-language professional publications. We matched these library journals with one Canadian information science publication (*Canadian Journal of Information Services*), five U.S. ones (*Journal of American Society for Information Science* [JASIS], *Information Technology and Libraries*, *Information Processing and Management*, *American Society for Information Sciences — Proceedings* [ASIS], and *Education for Information*), and one British journal (*Information Scientist*). We then randomly selected article titles from these journals (see Appendix B).

We first examined the titles of these articles in order to ascertain the range of topics that each of the two groups of periodicals covered during the same period, 1971 to 1991. We grouped these articles into discrete categories to assess the extent of the overlap between the information science and library science articles. We then devised a simple set of four categories to carry out our initial classification:

1. Library Literature: Content of articles focusing directly upon some aspect of institutional librarianship, the content of library work, problems of education for librarianship, as well as bookmaking, publishing, literature, rare books and media, and archives. Also included were discussions regarding general procedures for operating libraries and library networks.
2. Library Technology: Applications of computer and other electronically based technology to library work.
3. Information Science Literature: Content of articles focusing primarily upon issues dealing with the general nature of the communication of data and knowledge, including articles on information science and information technology, but excluding those that deal specifically with libraries and library networks.
4. Both: Content of articles concerned jointly with librarianship and information science, or information technology.

Findings

Our preliminary classification of article titles produced the array given in table 6. Ninety percent or more of the articles in library science journals are categorized as library literature for both the 1971-1981 and 1982-1991 periods. However, only 63 percent and 48 percent, respectively, of the articles in information science journals are classified as information science articles. While no more than 16 percent of the articles in information journals are categorized as library literature, the proportion increased to 24 percent (from 13 percent) in library technology and 17 percent (from 8 percent) in "both library and information literature."

TABLE 6. TYPE OF JOURNAL BY ARTICLE CLASSIFICATION OVER TIME[1]
1971-1981

Type of Journal	Article Classification				
	Library Literature	Library Technology	Both Library and Information Literature	Information Literature	
Library Science	91.2%	4.1	2.0	2.7	(147)
Information Science	15.7%	13.4	8.4	62.5	(83)

1982-1991

Type of Journal	Article Classification				
	Library Literature	Library Technology	Both Library and Information Literature	Information Literature	
Library Science	72.5%	16.8	4.6	6.1	(131)
Information Science	10.5%	24.2	16.9	48.4	(190)

Other[2]=7

The library-specific literature contained in library journals falls into standard categories that are quite stable across the two decades we are examining. In both periods (1971-1981/1982-1991), materials and

---

[1] Both patterns are statistically significant at the .001 level.

[2] We were unable to classify seven of the titles satisfactorily.

collections (16.2 percent/16.0 percent), library techniques and skills (14.7/12.6), library management (13.2/8.4), and library history (11.0/19.0) account for over half of the articles in this literature. We have displayed randomly chosen titles from each of these categories in table 7. The only notable difference, and it is a minor one, is that there are proportionately more articles (19.7 percent versus 7.4 percent) in the earlier period that can be clearly identified with specific library types (school, public, academic, special).

TABLE 7. RANDOMLY SELECTED LIBRARY LITERATURE TITLES IN LIBRARY JOURNALS

Materials and Collections		Journal
1971-1981	Alive and Well: the Contemporary British Novel (The status of contemporary British fiction is explored in Sheridan Baker's essay, "Alive and Well: The Contemporary British Novel," with his bibliographic selection of important titles for libraries.	*Library Journal*
	A Rationale for the Film as a Public Resource and Service.	*Library Trends*
1982-1991	Preservation Planning. Jan Merrill-Oldham Offers Ways to Strengthen Preservation Worldwide.	*Library Journal*
	Preservation Microfiche: A Matter of Standards.	*Library Resources and Technical Services*
Library Techniques and Skills		
1971-1981	Coping With Subject Heading Changes.	*Library Resources and Technical Services*
	Mr. Dewey's Classification, Mr. Cutter's Catalog, and Dr. Hitchcock's Chickens.	*Library Resources and Technical Services*

Table 7 — <u>continued</u>

1982-1991	Document Delivery Comes of Age in Pennsylvania.	*Wilson Library Bulletin*
	The Library of Congress Schedule: It's Time for a Change.	*Library Resources and Technical services*
Library Management		
1971-1981	Upping the State's Ante for Libraries.	*Library Journal*
	Analysis of Cost and Performance.	*Library Trends*
1982-1991	Library-Vendor Relations: An Era of New Challenges. Library-Vendor Relations Take on New Dimensions in an Automated Environment.	*Canadian Library Journal*
	Up the Beanstock. Presenting an Evolutionary Organizational Structure for Libraries. (Authors Irene B. Hoadley and John Corbin Offer a New Approach that Could Help Research Libraries Face the Challenge of the 1990s.)	*Library Journal*
Library History		
1971-1981	Daniel Cort Gillman on the Formative Period of American Librarianship.	*Library Quarterly*
1982-1991	The Organization of Italian Libraries from the Unification until 1940.	*Library Quarterly*
	Medieval and Renaissance Manuscripts from the Library of Sir Sydney Cockerell (1867-1962).	*British Library Journal*

The information literature found in information journals has some standard categories, with automatic indexing and classification systems (15.1 percent/8.5 percent), theoretical aspects of information retrieval (15.1/9.6), practical aspects of information retrieval (18.9/16.0), and public policy (13.2/13.8) as four major dimensions that underlie this literature in both decades. In the first period, articles in these categories accounted for over 60 percent of the total, as opposed to slightly less than 50 percent in the second. Several titles from each of these groups are displayed in table 8. Three new categories of some significance emerged in the 1982-1991 period — education (11.7 percent), information and communications technology (10.6 percent), and artificial intelligence and expert systems (7.5 percent). Representative titles from these three new categories include Documentary Retrieval in Education, Part 1: C, 1920-1965 [Information Scientist], CD-ROM Software Architecture to Promote Interchangeability [Journal of the American Society for Information Science], Enhancing a Hypertext Application Using National Language. Processing Techniques [Information Scientist], respectively.

There are a number of inferences that can be drawn from the general patterns in table 6. First, the amount of overlap that has occurred is relatively modest. Furthermore, the overlap occurs more frequently in the "library technology" or "both library and information literature" categories than in the purer "library literature" or "information literature" categories. For example, the maximum value in the overlapping diagonal cells is 15.7 percent, as opposed to 24.2 percent in the intermediate cells. This suggests that the connections occur more on the margins than in the core of the two areas. In addition, the substantial amount of overlap in the library technology area suggests that much of the commonality is about practical, technological matters rather than about shared theoretical perspectives. Finally, the amount of change over the two separate decades we examined is quite small. This indicates that if one wishes to apply the term "convergence" to the trends, one must do so with the understanding that the change is coming quite slowly. The one shift that deserves closer examination is in the "both library and information literature" categories. The increase of 8.5 percent between the two decades (16.9 percent versus 8.4 percent) is reasonably small, but it should be the location, if anything is, of convergence tendencies.

An examination of titles and abstracts for all articles classified in the "both library and information literature" category for the two periods

TABLE 8. RANDOMLY SELECTED INFORMATION LITERATURE TITLES IN INFORMATION JOURNALS

	Title	Journal
Automatic Indexing and Classification Systems		
1971-1981	Indexing Documents by Gedanken Experimentation	*Journal of the American Society for Information Science*
	Automatic Thesaurus Construction Based on Term Centroid	*Canadian Journal of Information Science*
1982-1991	Deriving Disciplinary Structures: Some Methods, Models, and an Illustration with Accounting	*Journal of the American Society for Information Science*
	A Generalized Database Directory for Nondense Attributes	*Information Storage and Retrieval (Information Processing and Management)*
Theoretical Aspects of Information Retrieval		
1971-1981	Relevance	*Journal of the American Society for Information Science*
	On Structuring the Archival Repository for Scientists' Machine-Readable Models	*American Society for Information Science - Proceedings*
1982-1991	Entropy and Information: A Multidisciplinary Overview	*Information Storage and Retrieval (Information Processing and Management)*
	The Application of Search Theory to Information Science	*American Society for Information Science - Proceedings*
Practical Aspects of Information Retrieval		
1971-1981	Searching Biases in Large Interactive Document Retrieval Systems	*Journal of the American Society for Information Science*

Table 8 — <u>continued</u>

	Practical Aspects of Information Retrieval	
	Researching Office Information Communication Systems	*Canadian Journal of Information Science*
1982-1991	The Operation and Performance of an Artificially Intelligent Key Wording System	*Information Storage and Retrieval (Information Processing and Management)*
	ONTERIS: Access to Ontario Education Information	*American Society for Information Science - Proceedings*
	Public Policy	
1971-1981	The Information Society: Where Consumerism and Cottage Industry Meet	*Canadian Journal of Information Science*
	International Data Communication Capabilities for Information Exchange Networks	*American Society for Information Science - Proceedings*
1982-1991	Section IV. NTIS-GPO: Federal Information Disseminators. The National Technical Information Service: A Federal Resource for Health and Information and Services.	*Journal of the American Society for Information Science*
	Linguistic and Political Barriers in the International Transfer of Information in Science and Technology	*Information Scientist*

under examination reveals several interesting trends. First, there is a major difference in attention given in the two periods to the nature of information systems. While six of the ten articles for the first period could clearly be considered expositions on the nature of information systems, this was only partly true for two of the thirty-eight articles in the second period. Whereas articles on "Different Dimensions of Information Retrieval" and "Mission Possible — A Future Information System" were to be found in the 1970s, the literatures had moved in the 1980s to a discussion of specific topics, dealing predominantly with issues like education for new systems, bibliometrics, and changing work environments. More typical titles, respectively, for the 1980s were

"Management Education for Archivists, Information Managers, and Librarians: Is There a Global Core?, Measuring the relative Standing of Disciplinary Journals," and "The Development of the National Research and Education Network." By the 1980s the routine nature of technological change in all areas of librarianship appears to have been accepted. The only general titles were futuristic ("Human evolution in space and time, with reference to the niches of librarianship and information processing") or semantic (A la recherche d'une définition des sciences de la bibliothéconomie et de l'information").

Conclusion

There are only some minor indications of technologically driven convergence in the professional literatures for library science and information science. The modest amount of convergence that does occur is located in the practical areas that touch on the utilization of the new technologies in different work settings. This small overlap is less about growing theoretical commonalities than about the similar impacts of new electronic tools that are found in distinct work settings. The evidence does little to encourage the view that we are looking at theoretical fields that overlap in significant ways, even in the longer term.

CHAPTER 5

LIBRARY AND INFORMATION WORK IN CANADA: ANALYSIS OF AN EMERGING LABOUR MARKET*

The definition of what constitutes a labour market, particularly in new or emerging areas of employment, depends to a large extent on the theoretical and conceptual assumptions of the particular investigation. Studies of the information and library employment market have been predominantly influenced by theories of postindustrial society that postulate the centrality of "information" for economic development in the present phases of the evolution of industrial societies. The well-known works of Bell, Machlup, and Porat have been especially influential in establishing general parameters for future trends. There has been relatively little empirical work done, however, on the nature of the specific emerging "information" markets that are of particular interest to the library profession.

In large measure this lacuna is the result of a confusion connected with the use and misuse of the pivotal term "information." This term has become so obscured by overuse and by imprecise definition that it has actually interfered with empirical investigations into the nature of the emerging information job market. In day-to-day conversation, precision of understanding is not crucial; one deduces general meanings from their context. But when discussing future job prospects of MLS/MLIS degree holders, or when making predictions about the future of the information profession, the practice of using the term "information," without first specifying what type of "information" is being referred to, has inevitably led to faulty communication and ill-fated policy decisions.

---

* Reprinted with permission from the *Canadian Journal of Information Science,* Vol. 16, No. 2, July 1991, pp. 40-51.

An illusion has been created that the MLS/MLIS degree holders can handle, with equal competency, the whole gamut of information activities that exist in postindustrial society. In fact, they are in good part educated to work with only a subset of these activities: the handling of bibliographic information, and the retrieval of factual data contained in text-based media. Semantic imprecision likewise makes it difficult to differentiate among the academic qualifications and practical skills that various types of information work require.   On the one hand, the capability of the MLIS degree holders to handle various types of information is overstated; on the other, an erroneous image is created of what the majority of them actually do.

Analysis of Relevant Research Literature

In the most comprehensive British study to date, Nick Moore (1987) undertook a careful empirical examination of the size of the emerging markets in the United Kingdom. Moore employed a keywords search of job advertisements in a broad range of newspapers and journals in February and May 1985. Specific descriptions were collected for "all advertisements which contained the key words — information, data, data-base, intelligence, library and advise, and any other which appeared to be relevant were also recorded" (Moore, 1987: 45). As indicated in the following listing (derived from Moore, 1987: 46-50), the jobs advertised were sorted into ten job types. Experts then sorted jobs in these ten categories into categories representing "established skills," "applied information work," "jobs requiring some other primary skill," and "information skills of no direct relevance" (the definitions of these labels are given in part B of the list).

A. JOB TYPES

Library Work

Jobs involving library, as opposed to information, skills or firmly based within a unit described as a library.

Information Work

Jobs requiring the fairly traditional skills of an information worker and usually based within an information unit or service.

Research and Information

Posts that, in addition to information work, required a fairly substantial element of research work. Such research work frequently required the collection of data from nondocumentary sources.

Information Technology

Posts that were primarily concerned with the use and application of information technology. Many of the posts in the emerging market as a whole require some familiarity with information technology. Posts included in this particular group were primarily concerned with the application of the technology itself.

Indexing and Abstracting

Most posts in this group were concerned quite simply with indexing and abstracting. Some, however, also included an element of technical writing.

Servicing the Information Library

This group was concerned with posts in the firms and organizations that service and support the overall information industry, for example, book selling and publishing when they were aimed specifically at the library and information market, bibliographic database suppliers, and library automation service.

Advice Work

This included the whole range of advice services from generalist agencies such as the Citizens' Advice Bureau to specialist agencies such as law centres, careers advice services, and independent advice centres.

Public Relations

Many public relations jobs were described as for an information officer. In some cases the work did involve the sort of skills possessed by an information worker; in most instances, however, the link was tenuous.

Management Information

Jobs int his group were primarily concerned with providing information about the internal operation of an organization. Usually this information was directed at the management of the organization and was used as the basis for decision making.

Records Management

Jobs in this group were primarily concerned with the organization, storage, and retrieval of files and other documentary records related to the work of the organization.

B. JOB CONTENT

Established Skills

These were jobs involving the practice of established library and information work skills. Usually these skills were called for in new contexts or in organizations that had not previously employed the librarians or information workers.

Applied Information Work

Posts in this category involved the development or novel application of library and information skills. In a sense, all jobs require the application of general skills to particular circumstances. Here, however, the jobs required the development of particular aspects of library and information work to the extent that they could be regarded as materially different.

Jobs Requiring Some Other Primary Skill

Applicants for these posts needed to possess some other primary skill, attribute, or qualification. It is likely, however, that the possession of library or information skills would have a direct application in the position and could very well enhance the chances of a candidate getting on to a short list for the job.

Information Skills of No Direct Relevance

These were jobs that appeared, on first glance, to be within the emerging markets, often because they included the word "information" in the job title. A closer inspection, however, revealed that they were either firmly within the province of another occupational group, such as career advisers or public relations officers, or that they called for a very high degree of specialist knowledge or experience. In such cases a library or information background would be seen as having very little relevance.

Data collection was then expanded to a full year (June 1984-May 1985) for five journals containing almost all of the jobs available in the first three of the four job content categories. Subsequent analysis of the entire year's advertisements produced a cross-classified table for job types and content (table 9). Of the 1106 jobs, 575 fall into the first three job content areas.

For Moore, it was crucial to distinguish between new jobs in the emerging markets that are predominantly computer or technology based, and new jobs more likely to be within the reach of a library school graduate. He maintained that "between librarianship and information science lies the third world of information work that is not technologically oriented or based" (1987: 38). The evidence he has provided makes it clear that job types such as "information technology" and "management information" do not constitute realistic markets for library school graduates (the job type of "advice work" is not relevant for other reasons). Moore estimates that 66 percent of category 2 jobs and 20 percent of category 3 jobs could be filled by librarians and information workers. According to Moore, these data mean that the emerging market in the United Kingdom is about 340 to 360 jobs annually, in addition to 1452 jobs in established markets (1987: 55). Using starting salaries as an indication of entry-level jobs, Moore estimates that only 40 percent of the jobs in emerging markets are open to new graduates. Employing a low 7.4 percent turnover rate for established jobs to project 10 percent or 12 percent turnover rates for the emerging markets, Moore estimates there are between 3000 to 36,000 emerging-market jobs, by comparison with 19,000 established ones. This means that the emerging market is between 15.8 percent and 19.0 percent of the size of the established market (Moore 1987: 87-89). Although one may have reservations about the methodological problems of using formal advertisements to define emerging markets, Moore's general patterns seem quite plausible and have received widespread acceptance in Britain.

TABLE 9.   JOB ADVERTISEMENTS IN THE
EMERGING MARKETS, JUNE 1984-MAY 1985

	Category				
	1	2	3	Total 1-3	4
Library work	75	5	—	80	7
Information work	127	18	17	162	7
Research and information		51	27	78	3
Information technology		15	29	44	209
Indexing and abstracting	1	4	10	15	13
Servicing the information industry		24	4	28	
Advice work		21	67	88	191
Public relations		12	10	22	48
Management information		18	24	42	60
Records management		15	1	16	
Total	203	183	189	575	531
	35.5%	31.8%	32.9%	100%	---

The North American literature on this topic is far scantier. In the United States, there have been frequent attempts to create profiles of "information professionals" based on varying conceptions of a growing "information economy" (Debons, King, Mansfield, and Shirey, 1981). At a more specific level, an analysis by Ching-Chih Chen, Susan Raskin, and Diane Tebbetts (1984) constitutes one of the few parallels to the Moore work, in terms of looking at market dynamics from the perspective of library and information schools. Chen, Raskin, and Tebbetts organized their research around a conceptual scheme similar to Moore's; they distinguished among "traditional," "technical," and "target" segments of the market (1984: 168). As they defined them, the traditional area consisted of jobs in "library-related fields," the "technical area" of jobs "which require specific technical training, such as computer software development," and the "target area" of jobs that "are judged by the researchers as suitable positions for our graduates."

Using Sunday advertisements from the two major northeastern papers, the *New York Times* and the *Boston Globe*, for two months (December 1982-January 1983), the researchers compiled a list of 549 available jobs: 66 were in traditional library areas, 93 in the target area, and the remaining 390 in the technical area. On the basis of a mail-back questionnaire to subsets of employers, Chen, Raskin, and Tebbetts created profiles of typical work settings.

By contrast to traditional jobs, which they found were located exclusively in educational and health services industries, the majority of the target jobs were, like the technical ones, located in private industry. The vast majority of jobs filled by organizations hiring in the target area involved analyzing and designing information systems (Chen, Raskin, and Tebbetts, 1984: 172). The job titles most frequently used to describe these jobs in both target and technical areas were "programmer," "software engineer," and "systems analyst." Their investigation suggested that the "target" or emerging jobs in the United States constituted a relatively smaller proportion of the "nontraditional market" than in the United Kingdom, and may be more closely tied to computer activities.

Similar work in Canada by Jack Duffy, Boris Raymond, and Richard Apostle (1989) suggested that the Canadian situation is closer to that in the United States than in the United Kingdom. Utilizing employment advertisements from the Toronto *Globe and Mail* for the January-December 1984 period, the authors selected all advertisements using such terms as "information," "systems analyst," "communications officer," "records manager," and similar phrases.

Duffy, Raymond, and Apostle conducted a mail-back survey of all employers (182 responses from 300 employers) to gather details on the jobs. They then employed library school students to develop a classification scheme for one-half of the 182 responses received and found that a reliable set of categories could be used to categorize the jobs being examined. Although only a small amount of information was collected in this survey, it was sufficient to enable the authors to identify a computer-based core of job skills for most of these positions. Further, they found that only a low proportion of MLS/MLIS graduates was being hired for them (see table 10).

In all three studies one is impressed by the lack of match between
employer expectations for "emerging" or "target" positions and the skills
possessed by typical MLS/MLIS degree holders. Moore, Chen et al.,

TABLE 10. RENAMED CATEGORIES AND FINAL RESULTS

	n	%	Successful candidates having an MLS degree %	Successful candidates having 1 or more years of formal computer education %	Successful candidates having 1 or more years of comptuer experience %
Programmer/ analyst	14	14.9	0.0	92.9	85.7
Manager of information systems/computer services manager	34	36.2	0.0	73.5	91.2
Public relations/ public affairs/communication	11	11.7	9.1	36.4	36.4
Records management/ health records administration	27	28.7	0.0	70.4	59.3
Miscellaneous*	8	8.5	25.0	12.5	12.5

* Two advertisements in this category had nothing to do with information jobs but were
in the original sorted sample to serve as a validity check and therefore these have not been
counted in this analysis.

and Duffy et al. all demonstrate for their particular countries that
relatively few MLS/MLIS degree holders are being hired in the new
market, and that their skills are not highly valued by employers who
operate in this market.

With a small but representative sample of the employers covered by his advertisements, Moore showed that "information work" qualifications are considered more important than librarianship qualifications. Further, he found that the highly ranked skills and experience, which here appeared to be more important than formal qualifications, seemed to focus primarily on the electronic aspects of the organization and retrieval of information and secondarily upon interpersonal skills. His parallel sample of individuals who successfully obtained jobs in the emerging market also showed that few employers considered formal education in librarianship to be particularly relevant. When they did give positive evaluations of the applicant's education, they identified courses in the organization of information (indexing, classification, cataloguing).

In a similar fashion, Chen, Raskin, and Tebbetts indicated that in the United States, while computer science was generally highly valued, an educational background in library and information science was typically viewed as the least relevant.

Duffy, Raymond, and Apostle, in their Canadian study, demonstrated that the majority of successful candidates for jobs that the advertising employers designated by such terms as "systems analyst" or "information officer" had more than one year of formal computer education and one or more years of computer-related work experience. Only three of the ninety-four Canadians jobs examined went to individuals with MLS/MLIS degrees.

Methodology of the Present Study

The aim of the current research project was to conduct a comprehensive national survey of "emerging information market" jobs listed in nine newspapers across Canada for the period from April 1, 1988, to April 1, 1989. The newspapers were the *Vancouver Sun*, the *Calgary Herald*, the *Winnipeg Free Press*, the *Globe and Mail* (national edition), the *Toronto Star*, the *Ottawa Citizen*, the *Montreal Gazette, Le Devoir*, and the *Halifax Chronicle-Herald*. Given limited financial resources, only the Saturday editions of these newspapers were searched, since they would yield the most advertisements for one particular day. An exception was the *Globe and Mail*, which switched its career section to Mondays, Wednesdays, and Fridays in January 1989; its Friday editions were selected from January 1989 forward.

The search was restricted to the advertisements that met the following criteria. (Note that criteria 3 and 4 were devised to exclude programmers/analysts.)

1. Any position that had anything to do with the storage, retrieval, dissemination, or creation of any type of information, excluding librarians employed by a library.
2. Positions that called for no more than five years of experience.
3. Positions that called for no more than one programming language (programming skills being peripheral to the position).
4. Positions that called for computer science graduates only were excluded.
5. Medical records positions were excluded if certification or the completion of a specific training course in the field was required.
6. Some corporate librarians were included on the grounds that the function of some corporate libraries is more like that of an information center.

By these procedures, 275 eligible advertisements were collected. Questionnaires were then sent in September 1989 to the organizations that had placed the advertisements, and 137 usable responses were received, virtually all by December 15, 1989. (Among the total responses received, thirty had to be rejected. The generous initial definition of "possible" advertisements meant, on detailed analysis, that nineteen individuals were found who should be classified as computer analysts, and nine who worked in a traditional library setting. Two others were excluded because they involved positions requiring more than five years' experience.) Given the lack of resources to do any follow-ups for the survey, the 49.8 percent response rate achieved was deemed satisfactory.[1]

Analysis of the Results

In keeping with their previous work, the authors grouped the 137 respondents into the four basic categories generated by their previous analysis (see table 10). This grouping yielded

1. Thirty-eight who were managers of information systems or computer services managers (27.7 percent);

2. Forty-nine who were employed in public relations and communications (35.8 percent);
3. Sixteen who worked as records managers (11.7 percent); and
4. Thirty-four who were in other kinds of related work (24.8 percent).

The types of job descriptions that were found to characterize these found categories confirmed the stability of the earlier typological construct (Duffy, Raymond, and Apostle, 1987).

The first category was a mix of computer services managers and managers of information systems. The second combined public relations with communications and some educational and training functions. The third, records managers, included just that. The fourth, or miscellaneous category, included research analysts, research associates/officers as the modal group, and three curators.

Although the categories developed by the Duffy, Raymond, and Apostle study remained consistent, there now appeared substantial differences in the proportion of the sample in each group. Specifically, there were considerably fewer records managers, somewhat fewer information managers, considerably more people in the public relations and communications fields, and somewhat more in the miscellaneous category. It was not possible to explain such a shift in proportion, since this particular survey was designed as a cross-sectional rather than a longitudinal study. One can speculate, however, that the new sample, being truly national rather than restricted to *Globe and Mail* advertisements, may reflect regional differences in employment market demands. This is clearly an area that lends itself to further investigation.

What was significant, however, was that the present study confirmed, with a high degree of correspondence, two important facts about the "emerging information market" in Canada. The first is that this market consists of several discrete categories that require quite different skills. The second pattern shows that, despite some significant differences, these Canadian categories are, on the whole, very similar to those found by independent research in Great Britain.

Further, this typology has proven itself to be particularly useful for illuminating the qualifications, skills, and experience regarded as essential by Canadian employers in the job market being studied.

As shown in tables 11 and 12, there are predictable patterns of characteristics associated with each job type. Information systems managers are expected to have computing credentials and skills and experience in computers, systems analysis, and organizing and retrieving computer-based data, as well as skills in interpersonal communication. Public relations employees are required to have credentials in journalism, or similar work, as well as skills and experience in writing and editing and in retrieving and organizing facts. Interpersonal communication skills are also important. Records managers are required to have skills and experience in organizing and managing text-based information as well as in archiving. The final miscellaneous category emphasizes "other" credentials (primarily social science degrees, particularly in economics and market research), research abilities, skills or experience in organizing and retrieving various types of data, and interpersonal communication skills.

TABLE 11. ESSENTIAL QUALIFICATIONS FOR THE 1988-1989 CANADIAN SAMPLE

	Information systems management (38)	Public relations (49)	Records management (16)	Miscellaneous (34)	Total (137)
Business studies	8	6	3	8	25
Computing	30	6	2	10	48
Information work	16	14	3	10	43
Journalism	0	10	0	0	10
Librarianship	3	1	1	0	5
Management	7	6	4	2	19
Public relations	1	8	2	5	16
Statistics	4	0	2	5	11
Other	2	12	5	14	33

TABLE 12. ESSENTIAL SKILLS AND EXPERIENCE
FOR THE 1988-1989 CANADIAN SAMPLE

	Information systems management (38)	Public relations (49)	Records management (16)	Miscellaneous (34)	Total (137)
Computer programming	19	2	0	7	28
Systems analysis	22	1	2	5	30
Use of computers for information work	26	16	6	13	61
Management	7	7	4	5	23
Office administra-tion	3	8	5	4	20
Typing	4	8	5	4	21
Journalism	0	10	0	1	11
Press and public relations work	1	14	0	4	19
Writing and editing	7	32	3	10	52
Advice work	4	9	4	4	21
Statistics	4	2	2	9	17
Research	6	12	4	15	37

Table 12 — <u>continued</u>

Organiz- ing and retrieving informa- tion	18	25	10	18	71
Librarian- ship	3	1	2	1	7
Records manage- ment and archives	8	4	12	4	28
Training	8	6	3	6	23
Interper- sonal commun- ication	31	36	11	25	103
Other	3	10	1	6	20

Overall, the data from the present survey stress the importance of computer-related abilities for the first job category, and the centrality of organizational and retrieval skills (as well as interpersonal communication skills) for all jobs except records management. The survey also confirmed data previously obtained, which showed that there was little demand for library credentials or skills for any of these positions.

Discussion

Labour market analysis in the newly emerging "information" field is currently beset by a variety of problems. On the demand side, differing theoretical and conceptual schemes have produced markedly divergent assessments of the nature and size of the job market in this area. On the supply side, the lack of fit between the expectations of employers operating in new markets and the typical educational backgrounds of MLS/MLIS degrees holders has reinforced a tendency to define potential new labour markets in vague and imprecise ways.

Library and information schools in North America, with some notable exceptions, have not responded to the challenges of these new markets by substantially altering the actual content of their curricula. Renaming library schools to incorporate an information dimension, and making modest revisions to curricula to incorporate some computer literacy and on-line searching courses, do not appear to be enough to meet the quite distinct trends of the traditional library and of the emerging "information" market.

Given the disjunction between "information" market employers, expectations and the skills of MLS/MLIS graduates, which the above data illustrate, the future response of schools granting those degrees to new market forces will be of considerable significance. The response to date — the minor changes in name and in curriculum suggested above — does not appear to be sufficient. The fact is that library and information skills are not perceived by the majority of the "emerging market" employers as being relevant to jobs in their area.

Nevertheless, Chen, Raskin, and Tebbetts Still maintain that a "major public relations campaign is necessary" (1984: 183) and could substantially alter employer perception of the suitability of MLS/MLIS graduates. Such beliefs are probably based on an unwillingness to differentiate among the various meanings involved in the "information" concept and the many different skills required by the "information" market. They stand in sharp contradiction to the findings reported in this study, as well as to the practices of many British educational institutions and of the University of Toronto. These schools have been moving, in the last several years, in the direction of differentiating traditional library education from that required by the emerging "information" markets. Thus one British information educator, Blaise Cronin (1987: 1), argues that the "spectrum of functions" performed and the "range of skills" exercised by the community of information workers are so "diffuse" that we must begin to recognize "quite fundamental intra-group differences in outlook, background and orientation."

If confirmed by further research along the lines of that presented here, such an internal differentiation means that it is unrealistic to expect that schools will be able to continue supplying their traditional library markets and at the same time compete with some of the jobs in the "emerging information" market if they offer only one curriculum. Rather, they are going to have to determine realistically the specific market niches they intend to occupy, and concentrate on realistic measures to meet the requirements of their chosen niches.

Notes

1. This conservative rate is calculated after removing the thirty unsuitable replies (from the 275 possible responses).

CHAPTER 6

LIBRARY AND INFORMATION SCHOOL GRADUATES AND THE EMERGING INFORMATION MARKET IN CANADA*

Introduction

The general concern of this chapter is with the nature of the demand for employment of librarians within the so-called information society. Its specific focus is on the "emerging information market" jobs that may be readily available to M.L.I.S. degree holders, and on the skill content of nonlibrary positions available to such individuals. One key proposition of the information paradigm (Apostle and Raymond, 1986) asserts that a large-scale transfer of work is currently occurring for holders of the M.L.I.S. degree. Such a transfer is said to be from work within libraries to a newly emerging market for information professions outside of libraries. Although often reiterated, this proposition seldom spells out what such work entails, except by citing examples from individual careers (Sellen and Berkner, 1984).

In order to test empirically the validity of this important assertion regarding the future career possibilities for graduates of library and information degree programs, it is necessary to find out what specific clusters of skills are most often sought in the "emerging information job market," to subdivide this sector of employment into its several components, and then to ascertain how many of the current library school graduates (M.L.I.S. degree holders) are actually equipped with

---

*

Reprinted with permission from the *Canadian Journal of Information Science*, Vol. 15, No. 1, April 1990, pp. 21-36.

such skills.

The Literature Survey: Some General Remarks

Most of the material found in an extensive literature search that was conducted on this topic, with the exception of the few empirical studies cited below, consisted of anecdotal writing or unsupported opinions. Dozens of articles stressed the bright employment prospects for M.L.I.S. degree holders in the information-related, nonlibrary field, with readers being asked to believe that the library and information field is a profession that plays a key role in modern society (Anderson, 1985). It is also frequently claimed that recent trends for employment of librarians have been in the direction of "nontraditional" careers and that employment prospects in abstracting and indexing "is where the action is" (Sellen and Berkner, 1984: 204).

Unfortunately, very little empirical research has been available to substantiate the reality of this optimism. Nor has there been much specification found concerning the skill content expected by employers from job applicants for such positions, or what proportion of them are being filled by M.L.I.S. degree holders, rather than by graduates from other professional disciplines such as computer science or business administration.

Placements in Library and Nonlibrary Jobs for M.L.I.S. Degree Holders: Some Statistical Data

Although there has been little empirical evidence presented to date (Duffy, Raymond, and Apostle, 1989), hopeful predictions have been made in Britain and the United States that one can anticipate the growth of an "emerging information job market" for jobs to which M.L.I.S. degree holders will be suitable (Debons, King, Mansfield, and Shirey, 1981; Moore, 1987). To this proposition has been added the recommendation that graduate library and information schools should enhance such employment prospects of their students by developing a better method of publicizing the skills of their M.L.I.S. graduates (Chen, Raskin, and Tebbetts, 1984). There also have been several Canadian studies done that attempted to deal with the question of an "emerging information market" from the perspective of past employment of their M.L.I.S. degree holders.

These studies reported slightly varying figures, but they all find that M.L.I.S. graduates who find full-time, permanent professional work outside of libraries are a small minority. Using placement data, Jean Tague and Jill Austin (1986) have found that less than 5 percent of Western's M.L.I.S. graduates from 1979 to 1984 obtained employment in the information sector. A 1982 University of British Columbia employment survey indicated that some 11 percent of its graduates for that year were employed, but not as librarians (Stuart-Stubbs, 1982). In a survey of the 1985 graduates, this proportion had dropped to 7.8 percent, with 5.8 percent employed not as librarians, but seeking a library position, and 2.0 percent employed not as librarians and not seeking a library position (Stuart-Stubbs, 1985). Miriam Tees (1986) reported that less than 12 percent of the 1984 and 1985 graduates from Canadian library schools found jobs in "nontraditional" settings.[1] The figures reported by a Dalhousie Library School survey in 1984 indicate that some 10.3 percent of alumni were engaged in full-time professional work involving library skills, but not in libraries (Apostle, Raymond, and Smith, 1984: 6-7). Roma Harris and Joanne Reid (1988) utilized job advertisements compiled at Western for 1980-1981 and 1985-1986 to show that since,

> the beginning of this decade there has been a slight decrease in the number of general, reference, acquisitions, and audio-visual librarian positions and a larger decrease in the number of advertised vacancies for teacher-librarians. The positions advertised for children's librarians, systems librarians, and information officers have increased slightly. (1988: 20)

This study also showed that if one adds the three categories that are not library-specific, "records management" (6.0 percent), "information officer" (4.1 percent), and "researcher" (2.1 percent), a total of 12.2 percent "nonlibrary-specific" positions were advertised during the survey period. Thus their figures for nonlibrary positions were close to those found by the other Canadian studies cited. Therefore, whether one uses job advertisements or placement information, all available Canadian studies suggested that less than 15 percent of recent graduating classes have found employment outside of the institutional library setting.[2]

Taking this as the point of departure, it is possible to argue that the current emphasis in library literature on prospects for employment of

MLS degree holders outside of libraries, in an "emerging information job market," creates an unrealistic set of expectations. This is especially so, since much of this employment outside of libraries is not located in the "emerging" market at all.

The Content of the Nonlibrary Positions Available to M.L.I.S. Degree Holders

Statistics cited above clearly indicate that nonlibrary jobs are but a minor part of the total employment market for library school graduates. Additionally, they do not constitute a single whole. Rather, they consist of many different kinds of work. Here the ambiguity of the nomenclature used in the literature is a source of confusion. Thus, besides "information professional" and "information manager," over a dozen terms are used as synonyms for an alternative or nontraditional career. Among them are database manager, indexer/abstractor, information counselor, information officer, information scientist, information systems analyst, records manager, and systems analyst.

The second area of terminological ambiguity concerns the definition of an "alternative" or "nontraditional career." In order to avoid the existing confusion, the present research was based on a specific definition. Its focus was full-time (not part-time), permanent (not contract or term), employees holding an M.L.I.S. degree who were not working in an institution properly called a library or school media center. This definition therefore excluded jobs in university, public, school, or special libraries.[3]

Aim of Study

The purpose of the present study was not to establish reliable estimates of total numbers of librarians working outside of libraries in Canada in 1988, nor to project the relative growth rates of this group. Such an effort would have required a study beyond the resources available. Rather, the purpose was twofold. The first was to establish, in as detailed a manner as possible, the specific types of work done by the group of full-time permanent employees holding an M.L.I.S. degree who were not working in an institution called a library or school media center. The second purpose was to study in detail those individuals who held positions that belonged to what the literature refers to as the "emerging information job market," (Moore, 1987), or the "target group" (Chen, Raskin, and Tebbetts, 1984).[4]

Methodology

In order to assemble a group of respondents who fit the above parameters for the study, one of the authors contacted the directors of the seven Canadian library schools in 1987 for the purpose of identifying recent graduates (1982-1986 inclusive) who they believed were working outside formal library settings.[5] Several directors supplied names directly; the majority chose on confidentiality grounds to send explanatory letters and return postcards (provided by the authors) to their own students. The estimate is that 241 people (including twenty-one individuals whose names were given directly to the authors) were sent letters asking if they would be willing to participate in the study. Ninety individuals indicated their willingness to participate. Subsequently sixty-eight completed surveys were obtained from the ninety individuals. These sixty-eight completed questionnaires have been used as sources for the data in the analysis presented below. The total response pattern was roughly proportionate by school attended and by geographic area. The directors who mailed out the 220 introductory letters to their students informed us that some of these individuals would currently be employed in libraries, might not be working at all, or may never have worked outside of libraries. Thus, we can not regard the 241 people who were sent introductory letters as an accurate estimate of the relevant population. We interpret the fact that eight of our sixty-eight respondents are currently employed in institutional library settings as partial confirmation of the potential nature of our nonresponses.

It was known, both from the literature reviewed and from personal observation, that a proportion of nonlibrary employed M.L.I.S. degree holders had taken positions completely (or partially) outside of the focus of their M.L.I.S. professional training, such as that of a cultural attaché in a Canadian embassy or a foreign language teacher.

The first task was to develop a typology that would help organize the wide distribution of jobs that was uncovered. In order to do this, it was first necessary to screen out (from the set of sixty-eight respondents) those individuals who were found to be currently working in the institutional library setting (eight respondents) as well as those who had acquired their library education prior to 1982 (two people). The remaining fifty-eight respondents were then sorted into the following four categories.

1. MAJORITY (fourteen cases). Individuals, the majority of whose work (51 to 100 percent) involved library-related skills. Example: teaching in a library school.
2. SOME (24 cases). Individuals, some of whose work (11 to 50 percent) involved library-related skills. Example: service representative for a library supplier.
3. NONE (thirteen cases). Individuals, little or none (10 percent or less) of whose work involved library-related skills, nor primarily related to computer technology. Example: accountant.
4. HIGHTECHS (seven cases). Individuals, little or none (10 percent or less) of whose work involved library-related skills, but was directly related to computer technology. Example: programmer for a computer firm.

It was decided to separate the HIGHTECHS from the NONES because they represented a quite distinctive subset of the general group that makes little use of its library training. These individuals, as the discussion below will show, spend a high proportion of their time performing fairly advanced tasks involving computer technology, and differ in other important ways from the remaining categories. We thus found fourteen, twenty-four, thirteen, and seven respondents, respectively, in the four enumerated categories, for a total of fifty-eight cases.

General Findings[6]

This typology was found to be helpful in explaining some important internal variations in the basic patterns that were identified as applicable to M.L.I.S. graduates employed outside the institutional library settings.

Relevance of Prior Experience for Current Job

In terms of experience prior to entry into library programs, the members of the SOME group were particularly likely to have been involved in the supervision or the hiring and training of staff, as well as policymaking and planning. It should also be noted that a considerable portion of our respondents entered their M.L.I.S. programs with prior work experience, some of which is related to computer-based work. Forty-three percent of them had some form of work experience before taking their M.L.I.S. programs, and an appreciable minority of these (over 30 percent) had done data or information preparation or analysis on behalf of others. A smaller minority (20 percent) had experience in systems analysis, or the management of information programs, services, or databases.[7]

Relevance of the M.L.I.S. Degree for Current Job

In terms of the relevance of library training to their current jobs, over 90 percent of the respondents stated that it was directly relevant, but 47 percent of these also admitted that individuals who had no M.L.I.S. degree could do the job "equally well." As one might expect, those who stated that their current work involved some, or a majority of library skills, were considerably less likely to state that individuals who lacked an M.L.I.S. degree could do the work as well as they did. Only 36 and 38 percent, respectively, of the MAJORITY and SOME groups, as compared to 62 and 71 percent, respectively, of the NONE and HIGHTECHS, thought that it is possible for those without the degree to do their jobs equally well.

In terms of training acquired prior to their current job, a considerable minority (over 43 percent), or even a majority (for the SOME group, not the HIGHTECHS) of all our groups except the MAJORITY one, reported having a year-long course in computer science. Only two of the twelve MAJORITY members group had at least a formal twelve month computer course. This pattern suggests that all of the groups, except the MAJORITY one, were inclined to obtain some computer skills before entering the nonlibrary job labour market.[8]

Placement to Current Job

There were some interesting overall patterns in the ways respondents obtained their current jobs. Fifty percent indicated that they had made applications to organizations in response to advertisements, 25 percent had utilized school placement bulletins or faculty contacts and referrals, and another 25 percent reported that they had obtained their jobs through friends, relatives, or through prior work connections. HIGHTECHS were more likely to use personal or previous work contacts to locate their current employment, while the SOME and MAJORITY groups were more apt to utilize library school staff referrals or school bulletins. The NONE group was most likely to use formal, external paths to employment. This contrast was compatible with the notion that faculty connections still run in more traditional directions, with the HIGHTECHS and the NONE groups having to turn to other means to find new forms of employment.[9]

Computer Content in Current Work

A large majority (over 79 percent) of the respondents did at least some work with computers in their present job. However, the proportions of total work time that involved computers differed considerably. In fact, there was a bimodal distribution for the respondents, with one substantial group reporting little or modest involvement, and another stating that they did a majority of their work with computers. Thirty-five percent of the respondents stated (forty-five respondents) that they devoted 25 percent or less of their work time to computers, while another 30 percent reported that over 75 percent of their work involved computers. There was a corresponding split in the respondents' descriptions of the optimal amount of computer training for the jobs they were currently doing. Thirty-five percent of those who did at least some computer work (forty-five respondents) stated that on-the-job training sufficed for them to learn their jobs. By contrast, there were six people, or 13.3 percent, who stated that at least a one-year course in computer science was necessary, and a further six who stated that a Bachelor of Science in computer science was required.[10]

The general structure of the typology used was partially validated by responses concerning the extent to which current jobs involved work with computer systems. While over 61 percent of all groups reported such involvement, all of the HIGHTECHS indicated that over three-quarters of their time was devoted to computer work. Forty-eight percent of the SOME group stated that over 50 percent of their work was done with computer systems. Only one person in the MAJORITY group and five in the NONE group had a similar level of work involving computer systems.

Gender and Income Relevance

There were two background factors that were relevant to the profile of work in the nonlibrary field for M.L.I.S. degree holders. First, over 41 percent of the individuals in the sample studied were males. This stands in fairly marked contrast to the typical composition of library school classes, where 80 percent or more of the class are women. Second, the salaries associated with work in the nonlibrary areas are comparatively high, with over half of the respondents indicating a 1987 gross income over $30,000, and 35 percent over $35,000.

There was a further strong connection between gender and predominant group location, with the jobs having some library content being more likely to be occupied by women. As shown in table 13, twelve of the fourteen members of the MAJORITY group were women, while six of the seven HIGHTECHS were men.

These gender and income patterns raise some important questions about the recruitment of new students and the implications of shifting the content of M.L.I.S. programs.

TABLE 13. TYPOLOGY BY GENDER

Type	Gender		
	Women	**Men**	
MAJORITY	85.7%	14.3	(14)
SOME	70.8%	29.2	(24)
NONE	30.8%	69.2	(13)
HIGHTECHS	14.3%	85.7	(7)

A substantial association between typology location and income was also found, with over 54 percent of the HIGHTECH and NONE groups making over $35,000 in 1987, and 26 percent or less of the other two groups making $35,000 or more.[11]

It should also be noted that the typology suggests that the jobs the M.L.I.S. graduates had acquired were not a part of the more general information market the authors previously identified in Canada (Duffy, Raymond, and Apostle, 1989). Only 21 percent of the respondents defined their current employment as belonging in the dominant categories that comprise the broader national information job market: programmer/analyst, information systems management, public relations, or records management.

An "Emerging Information Job Market" for the M.L.I.S. Degree Holders?

After developing this general typology, and using it to structure and analyze the data collected on all M.L.I.S. degree holders working outside of libraries, an attempt was made to isolate those individuals in the sample who could justifiably be said to occupy positions in the "emerging information job market." A study by Jack Duffy, Boris Raymond, and Richard Apostle (1989) has already shown that the "emerging information job market" was not a homogeneous one, that there were several segments within that market involving a variety of skills and requiring different types of education and/or experience. It is also known that a majority of jobs within this market were not realistically accessible to individuals who held only an M.L.I.S. degree without additional job experience or educationally acquired skills. However, there were reasons to suspect that there were some "niches" within this total pool of "emerging information jobs" for which M.L.I.S. degree holders would qualify. The second part of the present study was designed to find out as much as possible about these "niches": what skills they required, what previous experience was asked for, and whether job holders had taken these jobs because no library work was available to them, or because they preferred such work.

In order to accomplish this, a sifting process of all four of the described categories was initiated. This was done in order to screen out all members of the sample who did not fall within the parameters for jobs that actually represent "emerging information jobs." First eliminated was the whole of the NONE group (thirteen cases) since, by definition, no individual in this group held a position required the skills provided by an M.L.I.S. degree. This group of jobs included, for example, a writer of financial reports and speeches in telecommunication, a record keeper primarily involved with writing up data, a civil service keypunch operator, a researcher and writer of procedure manuals, a planner and surveyor of educational curricula development in colleges and libraries, a registrar in a library school, a language instructor, an editorial worker with a book publisher, a foreign service officer engaged in political and social analysis, and a teacher of secondary languages. In many of the jobs held by this group, skills learned in library schools were described as being very useful, but not as being a prerequisite for employment (e.g., bibliographical skills in writing procedural manuals).

The HIGHTECHS group of jobs was also excluded. This was done on the grounds that the primary skills that an individual had to have in order to be considered for such a position were not provided by the established M.L.I.S. programs of Canadian library schools. Individuals in this group were predominantly working on tasks that required a high level of computer technology skills, only a part of which could be acquired in an M.L.I.S. program. Therefore, the M.L.I.S. degree could not be considered as the essential prerequisite for such employment. At best, it would only be a useful adjunct to the other skills required, such as computer programming and the like. At the same time, the possession of a library school education (knowledge of the parameters of the field, its general needs, and its vocabulary) could be of some use to them as a "bridge" to potential library customers. As with the NONE group, almost every job in this group was unique. Some examples are: the management of systems and supervision of subordinates database design and customer support work, consulting on hardware and software support and development problems, programming for "customer interfacing," and programming, data analysis, and report writing.

From the MAJORITY group, those individuals were excluded who worked in long-established library-related organizations such as cataloguers for UTLAS, and in commercial library service organizations such as wholesale book dealers (Baker and Taylor), and who were involved in the performance of long-established library tasks such as cataloguing. These organizations have all existed for several decades and therefore did not fit into the definition of the "emerging information job market."[12] Other cases were also eliminated if they did not represent "emerging jobs," but rather consisted of traditional library-related work that has been performed for decades. These involved activities such as the servicing of libraries, instructing in library education, and providing consulting library service to special groups.

This left only three individuals from the MAJORITY category whose occupations could be considered as lying within the "emerging information job market." These were: working for organizations selling computer-related services to libraries and other organizations; performing information retrieval, indexing, and/or records management; and library-based research into information systems and bibliographic databases.

In the SOME group, there were several subgroups that could likewise not be associated with the "emerging jobs" market. The excluded subsets were:

1. Work involving primarily writing and editing. This subset was neither a new information field of activity, nor one for which one must have an M.L.I.S. degree.
2. Providing organizational management services. These jobs cannot be considered as being part of the new "emerging information market" because they are traditional managerial ones in which skills acquired in library school play only a subordinate role.
3. Providing library consulting services to special groups. This was also an old and well-established activity. It was certainly not an "emerging" one.

However, there were three subsets (twelve cases in all) were clearly part of an "emerging information job market":

1. Individuals whose work involved the building and/or managing of information programs and data bases as well as on-line searching (six cases);
2. The selling and servicing of database services to libraries and non-library organizations (five cases);
3. Providing research into information systems and bibliographic databases (one case).

These fifteen cases (three from the MAJORITY category and twelve from the SOME category) can be considered to be prototypes of the M.L.I.S.-dependent, "emerging information job market." They share certain commonalities:

1. All of them can be located within the fields, Nick Moore has identified as "information work" (see Appendix C).

2. Nine of these cases can be located within Moore's class, "servicing the information industry." All of these nine individuals stated that 50 percent or more of their work involved just four activities: (a) *marketing*, (b) *managing of information programs*, (c) *servicing databases*, and (d) *on-line searching and data or information preparation on behalf of others.*

3. The remaining five cases described their work as: doing information work (Moore's Class 2) — one case; information technician (Moore's Class 4) — one case; doing management information (Moore's Class 8) — two cases; and doing records and archival management (Moore's Class 9) — two cases.

4. Only 20 percent thought that it was possible to do their jobs equally well without the M.L.I.S. This clearly suggested that M.L.I.S. training was important for obtaining some jobs in the "emerging information market."

5. Eleven of the fifteen reported spending time doing on-line searches in their current job. By contrast, only five of the other forty-three individuals did any searching at all in their work. This was the most marked contrast among a wide variety of work tasks the respondents were questioned about. Since only two of the fifteen people identified with the "emerging information job market" claimed experience in searching prior to their M.L.I.S. training, there was a strong indication that this is the key area in M.L.I.S. education that was relevant to obtaining one of these "emerging information jobs."

6. Twelve of the fifteen in the selected subset were women. While this proportion was what one would expect for the MAJORITY and SOME groups, it did raise the prospect that, unlike the HIGHTECHS, (where the vast majority are males), there did exist places in the "emerging information market" where women with M.L.I.S. degrees could find employment.

Summary and Conclusion

This preliminary survey, together with its accompanying literature search, was designed to assess the employment opportunities outside of libraries that are available to holders of the M.L.I.S. degree in Canada. The conclusion that emerges from data presented above is that, to date, very probably less than 15 percent of recent graduates from the schools of library and information science have found employment outside of the institutional library setting within the first five years of receiving the M.L.I.S. degree.

The second conclusion that is suggested by the data is that the specific skills obtained in the course of this particular degree program are of direct relevance only within a rather narrow band of the total spectrum of information-related jobs in Canada. For the majority of such positions, other skills, such as computer expertise, various subject specialties, or the training provided by the M.B.A. (Management Information Systems) degree appear to be of more direct relevance.

The initial four-category typology of nonlibrary employed M.L.I.S. degree holders proved to be informative in terms of understanding the relevance of prior experience and M.L.I.S. training, the notion of placement processes, and the connections between this general area of employment to gender and income. First, the individuals in this study, save for those in the MAJORITY group, came to their current jobs with considerable computer training and computer-based work. Second, those whose work utilized the least M.L.I.S. training were most likely to use outside paths to employment. The HIGHTECHS tended to look to prior work contacts or friends, while the NONES were more inclined to make formal, external applications for jobs. Third, computer-related current employment was concentrated, as one might expect, among the HIGHTECHS, but also among the SOME group. This latter group, as was discovered later, was the locus of jobs that could be clearly located in the "emerging information job market." Fourth, the best-paying jobs tended to involve the least M.L.I.S. training, and these jobs were disproportionately held by males.

An additional aim of this study was to differentiate among the variety of jobs occupied by holders of the M.L.I.S. degree who were not employed within the institutional library setting. Analysis of returned questionnaires suggests that a large majority of such individuals do not directly utilize M.L.I.S. acquired skills, or utilize only some of them, with their positions requiring that these skills be supplemented by other courses or other types of work experience.

Of those cases where the jobs required primarily M.L.I.S. — related skills, most appear to involve activities that had existed in essentially the same form for several decades, that is, before the advent of computer-based information technology and the "information age." Such jobs therefore cannot with any honesty be counted as forming part of an emerging information job market. In the present study only fifteen out of a total of fifty-eight cases, or one-quarter, could possibly be categorized as being "emerging information jobs."

Since there is strong reason to believe that the total number of non-library jobs occupied by holders of the M.L.I.S. degree does not exceed 15 percent of all recent library school graduates (since 1984), the indication is that less than 5 percent (one-quarter of 15 percent) of recent M.L.I.S. degree holders can be said to hold positions in the "emerging information job market."[13]

Such a low rate of nonlibrary information work for Canadian library school graduates, if it is confirmed by other and more comprehensive studies, would have major implications for several key areas of the library profession. It would certainly impact upon the expectations that may now exist among new recruits to the profession.

Notes

1. Tees also notes considerable variation from one school to another. In 1985, 25 percent of Toronto's Faculty of Library and Information Science graduates obtained nontraditional forms of employment.

2. The researchers have been able to collect the following additional figures for the placement of graduates at Canadian library schools:

McGill University: 1987: "Other" (nonlibrary) = 2/45 = 0.9 percent.

University of Toronto: 1987: "Full-time, part-time and temporary positions in other information areas" = 6/68 = 8.8 percent.

University of Toronto: 1987: "Permanent, full-time positions in other information areas" (non-library) = 4/40 = 10.0 percent.

University of Toronto: 1986: "Full-time, part-time, and temporary positions in other information areas" = 7/66 = 10.6 percent.

University of Western Ontario: 1987: "Information industry, computer industry, consulting and information brokerage" = 8/103 = 7.5 percent.

University of Western Ontario: 1986: "Information industry, computer industry, consulting and information brokerage" = 13/91 = 14.3 percent.

University of Western Ontario: 1985: "Information industry, computer industry, consulting and information brokerage" = 5/82 = 6.1 percent.

University of Western Ontario: 1984: "Other, e.g. information industry, computer industry, freelance, community information centres, etc." = 6/98 = 6.1 percent.

University of Western Ontario: 1983: "Other, e.g. information industry, computer industry, freelance, community information centres, etc." = 6/84 = 7.1 percent.

The sources for these data are the McGill University Graduate School of Library and Information Studies, the University of Toronto, Faculty of Library and Information Science, and the University of Western Ontario School of Library and Information Science.

3.   In the data analysis below, we analyzed each case individually for corporate or governmental "information centers," where such centers may or may not actually be special libraries operating pseudonymously.

4.   The "target group" was defined as "positions which fit into the Debons-King categories and are judged by the researchers as suitable positions for our graduates" (Chen, Ruskin, and Tebbetts, 1984: 168).

5.   From a methodological viewpoint, it would have been preferable to study all graduates for the time period selected, and to study graduates over a longer period of time. However, the costs involved in these expansions of our study design far exceeded our limited funding. The researchers therefore resorted to asking the seven library school directors to provide names of (or to contact themselves) any of their graduates who they thought would fit the criteria of the study.

6.   Although we have only a modest sample size, we have chosen to present our data in percentage form to facilitate relevant comparisons. Readers should keep our small database in mind when assessing the qualitative patterns discussed.

7.   Twelve people report having other graduate degrees. Five have master's degrees in humanities, three have master's in social science disciplines, two have doctoral degrees in English, and one has a doctoral degree in sociology. The twelfth person has a law degree. Two-thirds of the respondents with graduate degrees outside library or information science state that their other degrees were "somewhat important" in getting their jobs.

8.   None of our seven HIGHTECHS has another graduate degree, while four members of each of the other groups have other graduate degrees.

9.   This is not to suggest that faculty members may not be instrumental in encouraging students to seek new forms of employment.

10. Six of the seven HIGHTECH respondents reported that 76 to 100 percent of their job time is spent working with computer systems.

11. For the purposes of this study, a job only qualified as being part of the "emerging information market" if it did not exist, under the same or another name, before the development of commercially available computer technology, that is, before the middle sixties.

12. Because the sample was small, it is quite possible that other "emerging information market jobs" may exist that this sample did not capture. This may especially be the case with certain rather unique occupations, such as "information brokers." However, according to informal but reliable information we have obtained, there are fewer than fifty full-time individuals in all of Canada whose work, because of the utilization of computer technology, involves functions qualitatively different from those performed by the ages-old freelance librarians and contract researchers.

13. This category, as defined above, is clearly not identical to the "nontraditional jobs" category sometimes referred to in library literature. There are a number of such "nontraditional jobs" within library institutions, especially within the small special library group, which would be excluded by our definition of the "emerging information job market."

CHAPTER 7

CHANGES IN CANADIAN LIBRARY
AND INFORMATION SCHOOL CURRICULA
AND ORGANIZATION DURING
THE PAST TWENTY YEARS

In order to evaluate the effectiveness of Canadian LIS schools in providing their students with an education that would enable them to successfully compete for jobs in the current employment market, it is necessary to separate the traditional institutional library employment market and the hypothesized new, nonlibrary field of employment in the "emerging information market" that is said to be developing in the government and private sectors of the Canadian economy. There is little criticism of the LIS school curricula when it comes to the provision of knowledge and skills for the first market. Over the many years since Dewey, library schools have gradually evolved a curriculum that adequately serves its needs, as well as developed institutional safeguards such as the A.L.A. accreditation procedures. Nor is there much criticism of the seven Canadian schools for the current slump in demand for new librarians; these demands are recognized as products of economic and social forces beyond school control.[1]

What we need to do is examine the extent, if any, to which Canadian LIS schools have shifted their curricula in order to accommodate the presumed new development of a noninstitutional library employment market. In order to evaluate this shift, the authors conducted an in-depth study of the latest calendars of all seven schools, and also visited each of them in order to interview their faculties. These visits took place in the spring and fall of 1992.[2]

In examining the seven programs, we paid particular attention to the ways the schools altered or added to their curricula in order to meet these new "information market" needs. Here we specifically focused upon two major variables: the direction in which the schools had moved in order to incorporate the skills required by the new computer technologies ("information technology") (Daniel, 1987) and, secondly, the extent to which they infused their curricula with "information science" courses such as database construction and bibliometrics, as well as the extent to which they had introduced courses dealing with various forms of "grey literature" and nonbibliographic "information services" that are an essential component of many of the nonlibrary "information" jobs.

Besides these key questions that relate directly to the issue of the capability of Canadian LIS schools to provide an education that would expand the employment prospects of their students beyond the traditional library employment market, we also attempted to determine whether new faculty members are being recruited to help build up the "information" components of these programs, and whether adequate equipment and laboratory resources were being made available to expand training in these areas.

In order to conduct our analysis, we first developed a model of a traditional core curriculum, and utilized it as a benchmark to discuss subsequent changes that were introduced into LIS school curricula. For this purpose we used the early 1970s as a starting point. This date was a convenient one because all seven Canadian schools moved to a two-year master's degree program at that point (McNally, 1993),[3] making it possible to set up a basic four-square curriculum design that closely reflected the prevailing curricula of the seven schools.

The Traditional Core Curriculum

What we found was that most of the Canadian LIS programs offered classes in collection development, cataloguing/classification, reference, and administration as the foundation of their curriculum. There were variations on this structure, with some of these topics being subsumed by other classes, or offered as electives.[4] For example, in 1971-1972, the M.L.I.S. program in the School of Librarianship at the University of British Columbia (U.B.C.) required the following three courses, among eight first-year mandatory ones:

505.　Organization of Materials. The basic processes of developing library collections; bibliographical arrangement of library materials.

525.   Classification and Cataloguing. Principles and practice of bibliographic description and subject analysis of library materials.

520.   Information Services. Principles and practice of reference work; organization of information services in libraries of all types.

U.B.C. did not offer an explicit, stand-alone administration course. This concern was evidently handled in separate second-year classes on public, school, special, and university libraries.[5]

A major exception to this overall pattern was the program at the University of Western Ontario. Western explicitly rejected this type of organization on the grounds that "professional theory and methodology is not taught by traditionally dividing the subject into courses devoted to book selection, cataloguing, classification, and reference" (School of Library and Information Science, The University of Western Ontario, 1971-1972). In addition to offering three required half-classes in professional theory and methodology, Western provided three further required half-classes in information and communication studies that were "concerned fundamentally with the knowledge and theory necessary for insight into the newly conceived discipline of information science." These classes included linguistic and communication studies, introduction to problems in the control of information, and problems in the computer control of information.[6]

Curriculum Changes Since the Early 1970s

By the mid-1990s the traditional titles and course descriptions of most Canadian LIS schools had been substantially altered, due primarily to the wide adoption of a new "information" nomenclature, one that has substituted such titles as "Organization of Information" for "Cataloguing," and "Information Services" for "Reference Services."[7] We also found that while a majority of Canadian programs have renamed their offerings to reflect their new concerns. By 1988, all seven Canadian programs had incorporated the term "information" in their units' title, with six of these changes occurring between 1982 and 1988. This renaming mirrored similar alterations taking place in the United States, and signaled a general concern to be identified with a potential growth area. However, two schools, Alberta and British Columbia, have maintained their traditional descriptions of the core curriculum, and a third, Western Ontario, has diminished the amount of information terminology that it employs.

Along with this trend, the organization by most schools of courses in "information technology" and "information services" has experienced considerable elaboration and diversification, such as the addition of courses in online database searching. As well, such housekeeping functions as computer-based processing of acquisitions and the utilization of machine-readable cataloguing data have also grown. All Canadian programs now have required courses in the area of "information technology," "information systems," and the like. Some of the courses in automation, data processing, and similar offerings were mandatory since the early 1970s.

The seven Canadian LIS schools all instituted computer courses by the early 1970s when computers became relevant to the processing of text-based materials (Large, 1993; Tague, 1979). The last twenty years have seen a number of developments in the familiarization of students with relevant computer hardware and software, as well as with the way to help library patrons utilize some of these tools.

At the University of Toronto, the M.L.S. program in 1991-1992 had six required half-classes. In addition to courses on the "Information Environment and Users" and "Research Methods," there were courses titled:

INTRODUCTION TO RESOURCES AND COLLECTIONS

An overview of the nature of library resources and collections. Literature searching, theory and practice is taught using both manual and machine methods to access the literature of librarianship. The course also introduces a theory of literature production, dissemination and use, and outlines the contribution of networks to total resources. Bibliographic control is the key issue discussed, with emphasis on national bibliography and international methods of achieving and promoting control.

ORGANIZATION OF INFORMATION AND MATERIALS

Principles and methods of organizing, describing and analyzing materials for the storage and retrieval of information.

LIBRARY ADMINISTRATION

The library as an organization and the effects of the administrative process on the provision of library service. Emphasis is on library goals and objectives, financial planning, theories of organizational behaviour and library personnel.

INTRODUCTION TO THE
TECHNOLOGY OF INFORMATION SCIENCE

The course provides an introduction to computer hardware and software with emphasis on minicomputers and interactive systems. It treats the new technological developments in the context of libraries and also more broadly in terms of their impact on society. Students are required to solve a set of library/information-related problems using a modern programming language.[8]

From the point of view of our research agenda, the key questions 116about the expansion of "information" content in Canadian programs devolve into an examination of the extent to which students are being exposed to computer systems and technologies as required for adequate on-the-job performance in the institutional library market, as well as in the perceived "emerging information market." In more practical terms, we were concerned with the adequacy of LIS preparation of their students to participate in the process of acquisition, storage, and retrieval of materials through the application of computer technologies.

Canadian library schools have all established computer laboratories for instructional purposes, and have staff who are capable of motivating students in current applications. However, as Large (1993: 24-25) points out, schools are currently being squeezed by the cost of quickly obsolete technologies and the frequent absence of technical assistance to maintain and upgrade laboratories. While this is a fairly common plight in many non-natural science units in Canadian universities, the relatively small size of library and information schools makes the tasks involved a substantial burden.

What is still not clear is the precise dimension of this change, specifically, what is the exit skill level of students who complete these courses, that is, do they go beyond teaching computer literacy? Do they provide students with a solid understanding of computer hardware and computer systems? Do they provide LIS graduates with skills that predominate in advertisements for the "emerging information market?" Do they enable students who do not intend to obtain jobs in libraries to compete on an equal footing with MBA/MIS graduates or with graduates of computer studies?

Our informants from Toronto and Western made the following points:

- Most of the students who enrolled in the Information Systems stream were already working in the field. In our first year we only admitted four students. After they finished a full year of the program they decided that they wanted to change to part-time status. Since then about 80 to 90 percent of our students have been part-time, and they almost invariably work for banks, insurance companies, or department stores. They are programmers, system managers, or database managers.

- Our (Toronto) computer science department considers itself very much a science. Until very recently they were not interested in users, per se. Studying users was all right, but it was not considered to be computer science. It was mainly focused on what happens inside a machine. By contrast, the Faculty of Library and Information Science are very much interested in users and user studies. The university has a computer science department and also an industrial engineering department, both of which offer very technical courses, while we concentrate on systems analysis and user studies.

There is considerable variation in the extent to which Canadian library and information schools have moved toward staking a claim to the "information science" end of the spectrum. On the one hand, there are units that, aside from courses dealing with computer technology, only extend their interests to established areas like indexing and abstracting and records management.[9] In the middle, there are schools that are moving into dealing with primary data, "grey" literature, audiovisual materials, and other nontextual artifacts that contain knowledge. The obvious practical limitation here is on the amount of preexisting knowledge and experience students must bring to the area. In the extreme, "subject specialists" sometimes require considerable formal education in related fields to benefit from such classes. Finally, there is the precedent of a stand-alone M.I.S. program at the University of Toronto.

Insofar as there are some overlaps with more traditional curriculum concerns, they tend to cluster intellectually around the notion of file structure principles that can be utilized to produce predominantly bibliographic retrieval systems for print and electronic media.[10] In general terms, "the core activity is determining what the specific needs are, how to develop structures in systems to satisfy those needs, and how to collect material or provide access to material." The notion of some convergence has led the University of Toronto to move toward a new master of information studies designation for a single, merged programme. While a specific information science package will be retained for those interested in systems analysis and mathematical foundations, the mainstream is also expected to become more technologically oriented.

To the extent that Canadian LIS schools are moving into the "information studies" realm, they are facing problems in delineating the boundaries of this "nontraditional" set of activities, and its connection to more traditional LIS focus. The theme around which much of the new "information" curriculum is being organized is that of "information management." As one of the interviewed faculty members put it, "We certainly see that in the private sector and in certain parts of the federal government the concept of "library" is gone...it is the conception of information management that is the key." Primary classes in this new area of concentration include records management, print and electronic records management, as well as database development.

Some members of the LIS faculties in Canada have claimed that graduates of M.L.I.S. program are to be preferred in many organizational contexts because their training has given them a greater sensitivity to user needs than that acquired by graduates of computer science, MBA/MIS, or engineering programs. As one faculty member phrased it, "Human-computer interaction...is not their main thrust. The recognition of users and user needs is much easier to establish in information studies than in computer science." While business schools can provide some of the same socialization, it is argued that they still concentrate on information as "information for managers."[11]

The principal rational for the contention that LIS graduates can compete successfully in the "emerging information job market" was given by several members of the Western and Toronto LIS faculties. It was based on the proposition that the LIS programs area able to instill a greater sensitivity to users' needs than the MBA/MIS or computer programs, as well as to better focus on what is really needed by users. These faculty members argued that because information management systems taught in business schools focus on management and profitability, rather than on access to internal and external information, they do not produce graduates with an adequate service attitude. With regard to graduates of computer science courses, their arguments ran as follows:

● Our focus here is on user involvement. While not something inherent, computer science departments in general don't focus on these things. The computer-science-trained people are much more knowledgeable about the hardware, but they don't always think about how people are going to use it. MBA/MIS departments are generally a much narrower subset of information courses than are courses in LIS schools because they have to focus primarily on information generated within an organization. They tend to look at a very narrow range of information.

● We have a course in database management systems. Any librarian who wants to stay current with what is happening has to know about that. Our graduates could go into any environment and establish their own systems, but if they go into a larger organization with a computer science department, it would be foolish for them not to use them. We also offer a course in software evaluation.

● Part of our task is having the marketplace understand what our graduates can do. We (Toronto) are currently beginning to integrate our program without giving up the separate streams. We want to have an umbrella degree with specializations. That has some special advantages, the first being that the way it is set up, now that these streams are completely separate.

● The content of the information science sequence and the target audience is a limited one. Its primary focus is on any type of information retrieval, and not only in bibliographic information. It focuses on general information systems. Mainly it is concerned with customizing systems for a particular organization, so that the emphasis is on working collaboratively with a user community in helping identify what their needs are, and bringing to bear their knowledge of how the work needs to be done. It focuses on software development companies that market library automation packages which provide programs for handling acquisitions, circulation, and so on. These have to be customized for particular installation. This course would be useful for someone who is on the technical systems side of the organization, and who wants to work closely with the user community in developing a particular information system. The content of the course does not necessarily focus only on a library-related environment.

The Organizational Level

At the organizational level, there have been only a few major developments. Canadian LIS schools have remained comparatively small units located in very diverse university settings. In 1991, they averaged only eleven full-time staff, with units ranging from seven to eighteen members. At the same time, the two Ontario schools were separate faculties, while the other five were connected to different academic units (Administrative Studies, Arts, Arts and Science, Education, Graduate Studies).

There are some significant regional variations in the institutional and socioeconomic settings for Canadian library and information schools. As is true for a number of related educational issues, professional schools located in closer proximity to the core of the Canadian economy tend to differ in systematic ways from those on the periphery. LIS units based in central Canada were the first to develop significant information components, and are the ones in which they generally have the highest profile. The two doctoral programs in the field are situated in Ontario, as is the only stand-alone M.I.S. program. While there may be some debate about the utility of having M.I.S. curriculum offered as part of a separate package of skills, it is nevertheless a partial expression of labour market and industrial realities that Ontario should have an M.I.S. program. The two Québec programs, and particularly the one at Montreal, are affected by the relative absence of public libraries as a potential source of employment. However, in general, this provincial difference tends to reinforce core-periphery distinctions because Montreal has tended to emphasize the western European documentalist tradition and a corresponding interest in special libraries. By contrast, the unit in British Columbia (with its Archieves component), as well as Alberta and Nova Scotia, have markets and environments that require some attention to local professional constituencies and employment opportunities in school and public libraries. Again, one can think of significant qualifications on this general point for virtually every school,[12] but the fundamental realities of Canadian political economy do confront each unit with external circumstances and constraints that they can ill afford to ignore. As one informant from a unit outside central Canada put it,

> "We do not have theoretical courses where information as such is abstracted from institutions or users. There is no indication of a market for this. We may be arch-conservatives, but our students must know libraries and how they work. It is a question of providing connections to libraries."

One major professional consideration all units have to face is the question of periodic academic reviews. In addition to the usual internal reviews that are conducted by home institutions, library and information units are subject to accreditation reviews every seven years by the American Library Association (ALA). The accreditation process involves the preparation of elaborate self-study documents, formal visits by ALA-appointed accreditation teams, and the eventual production of substantial final reports. While there is some recognition of the value of having external validation for a unit's activities, there is growing discontent in Canada with the amount of work required to fulfill review expectations. There is also some concern that the ongoing scrutiny to which library and information units are subject is inadvertently undermining the position of these units. Aside from the question of draining valuable resources into overly complex reviews, there is also some skepticism that a professional group that goes to such lengths to justify its credibility deserves closer observation.[13]

Finally, each of the library and information units has to deal with some ongoing incompatibilities between the educational and occupational backgrounds of their students, and the possibility of enhancing the information dimensions of the skill packages of their students. For example, one program still finds over half its recruits coming out of the humanities and social sciences with an "I like books and people" perspective, which makes the mandatory class in information technology a real trial for the majority of them.

Discussion

One of the questions that needs to be asked, but is frequently difficult to answer, is why certain things do not exist. Is it possible that the absence of certain curricular changes may be less a result of negligible environmental demands than of institutional inertia associated with generational differences in the bodies of knowledge they bring to the academy? Is it the genuine heterogeneity of the new labour market demands, and the corresponding differences in types of information being sought, that make it difficult to systematize new fields, or to popularize them?

A problem that needs to be addressed in this context is the connection, if any, between curriculum and the ability of a particular school to survive retrenchment exercises. The deepening recession has provided a backdrop for the actual closure of library schools in North America, but there is little evidence to date that financial cutbacks are directly responsible for school closures (Paris, 1988: 126).[14] Rather, isolation of schools within their own universities, along with an inability to articulate a persuasive sense of mission, make library and information schools vulnerable to closure. More specifically, schools that have curricula that are out of date, or are trying to make changes that are regarded as radical departures from the past, are susceptible to elimination (Paris, 1988: 143, 148-150). In terms that come from the sociology of professions, library and information schools may be engaged in losing "jurisdictional disputes" with other exclusive professional groups in management or computer science (Abbott, 1988). These other professions currently have some advantages in presenting claims to possessing a body of abstract knowledge applicable to this emerging information market. To the extent that these other professions have already established academic position, and to the extent that librarianship lacks an effective body of abstract knowledge, library and information schools may remain vulnerable.[15]

The suggestion here is that while LIS schools most certainly have to transform their curricula in order to accommodate themselves to a new computer and communications technologies, as well as to some modest possible expansion of the market for their graduates in the "emerging information field," they must be very careful not to lose their traditional institutional public, school, and academic library markets, markets that define them as a unique profession.

In the Canadian case, there is probably less to worry about in this respect than in the United States, because each of the LIS schools is part of a powerful, prestigious institution that has a wide array of graduate academic and professional program (McNally, 1993: 17). This favorable position, however, also presents a serious challenge for them with regards to their ability to generate a strong research agenda and thus make a serious contribution to a clearly demarcated academic field.

In addition, the seven Canadian programs are geographically distributed in ways that fulfill implicit regional mandates, a situation that probably adds to their relative institutional security.[16] However, the fact that most of the programs are relatively small and are attached to different faculties may be evidence of a lack of clarity about their missions and, in some instances, may leave the schools open to attack.

Finally, the seven Canadian schools, with the potential exception of Western Ontario, uniformly offer a two-year master's degree. This stands in marked contrast to the one-year norm in the United States, and provides an opportunity to include a larger spread of courses, a significant factor in rendering their graduates more competitive in the current job market.[17]

Having made these observations, it is still true, as the ALA Special Committee on Library School Closing indicates, that actions "directed at changing the overt characteristics ascribed to schools which have closed will not guarantee the viability of those which remain" (1991: 9). Combating "the aura of a waning profession" will take as many positive measures as defensive ones. Whether one can clarify a professional position, or change the image of a professional group, presents a vigorous challenge to many disciplines today.

Notes

1.   The one exception to this statement that we came across during our interviews was that there might be a slight overproduction of new degree holders, given the current market requirements.
2.   Boris Raymond visited McGill and Montreal in February 1992, and Richard Apostle went to Alberta, British Columbia, Toronto, and Western Ontario in April and May 1992. Boris Raymond returned to Toronto in October 1993, Western Ontario in October 1993 and April 1994, and British Columbia in June, 1994. The individuals we spoke to include the following:

Alberta	Sheila Bertram, Dean
British Columbia	Ken Haycock, Director
	Peter Simmons, Acting Director
	Basil Stuart-Stubbs, Former Director
McGill	Andrew Large, Director
	John Leide
	Peter McNally
Montreal	Paulette Bernhard
	Richard Gardner
	Paule Rolland-Thomas
Toronto	Adele Fasick, Dean
	Ethel Auster
	Joan Cherry
	Andrew Clement
	Joanne Marshall
	Charles Meadow
	John Wilkinson
	Nancy Williamson
	Karen Melville, Placement and Public
	Relations
Western Ontario	Dale Bent
	Gillian Michell, Associate Dean
	Roma Harris
	Catherine Ross
	Jean Tague, Dean

3.   McGill introduced a two-year M.L.S. degree without thesis in 1965 to provide a professional master's degree that would cover an expanding set of required and elective topics. Dalhousie, Montreal, and Toronto followed in 1970, with British Colombia in 1972 and Alberta in 1976. The University of Western Ontario adopted a forty-five credit, three semester system in 1967 that not infrequently ran into two years for completion (McNally, 1993: 14-16).

4.   A few of the core classes were already being given titles that incorporated "information" terminology, for example, "organization of information," and "information services."

5.   Although U.B.C. still does not place emphasis on distinct classes in the area, it did have a required first-year class entitled "Introduction to Automation" (535). This course was described as an introduction "to applications of computers and related equipment in library management

and bibliographical analysis."

6. According to one informant, this system broke down fairly quickly. An older organization based on classification, cataloguing, and reference and collections reemerged under the new categories. They "evolved back into the old system."

7. As Daniel (1987) points out, U.S. schools, like Canadian ones, have found the management category increasingly overlapping with courses given in business programs. The persistence of administration classes in library programs has as much, or more, to do with organizational boundaries between academic units as it does with the actual content of such classes.

8. The Master of Information Science program at the University of Toronto demanded more information science training of its students. Along with a research methods course, students in this program are required to take classes on the "Origins and Uses of Information for Databases," "Information Retrieval," and "Information Services Management." However, this twelve-month program typically attracted less than one-tenth the enrollment of the M.L.S. program.

9. This development may diminish direct overlap and competition with engineering and computer science as professions. Alternatively, schools that venture too far into these areas may incur the wrath of professions intent on maintaining traditional boundaries.

10. Systems can also be constructed for numeric data, graphic images, and the like.

11. Business people are also regarded as "very profit-oriented" or "entrepreneurial." "They don't have a service orientation."

12. British Columbia has a program in archival studies that has both a national and international audience; Alberta, while the only unit on the prairies, does not serve as "the prairie institution"; Dalhousie introduced information science ideas into its programming from the outset.

13. In the extreme, Alberta had to endure four major review exercises between 1986 and 1991, one of them an accreditation. The relatively small size of the unit was used as justification by an internal review for recommending that the faculty be restructured as a school for administrative purposes ("Maintaining excellence and accessibility in an environment of budgetary constraint." University of Alberta, Edmonton. February 1991).

14. Daniel (1986) does suggest that relative professional status may interact with financial pressures to make library and information schools vulnerable targets. Daniel (1986: 630) states, "In the library/information

library/information field the closing of one school precipitated a domino effect — i.e., a rash of closings around the country. In the national system of priorities, library/information schools were perceived to be weak and less able to defend themselves than other more prestigious disciplines and professions."

15. The ALA points out that many of "the universities which have closed their library schools offer other active and visible education programs in information science and specialized information handling subjects" (ALA Special Committee, 1991: 8). In addition, the Special Committee argues that adding the phrase "information science" to the names of library schools is insufficient. It has raised expectations which have not been fulfilled (1991: 7). Our ranking of Canadian schools produces only a .75 Spearman's correlation between the emphasis on information science in a program's description and its actual content.

16. In addition, one should be aware of a possible gender dimension. As the ALA notes, "Those professions deemed to be principally womens' fields still do not fare well in the academic world" (ALA Special Committee, 1991: 7).

17. McNally (1993:10-14) discusses the historical evolution of different postwar patterns in Canada and the United States. On the creation of a two-year master's program as a first professional credential, McNally comments, "There was a felt need to ensure a distinct difference between a graduate degree and a library technician's diploma; neither inside nor outside the universities was it generally appreciated that a BLS was a graduate degree."

CHAPTER 8

REFLECTIONS:
LIBRARIANSHIP IN A POSTMODERN ERA
(by Richard Apostle)

We are experiencing major transformations in the structure of the
complex economies and societies in North America and western Europe.
We may, in fact, be witnessing organizational and technological changes
of the same order as the industrial and democratic revolutions that gave
rise to modern society. While we are uncertain about the direction of
changes (Will they increase individual or collective well-being? Are
they progressive in nature?) as well as the magnitude (Are the changes
cumulative? How thoroughly will they affect social relations?), the
social sciences are taking the new problems very seriously. We have
created a new vocabulary to discuss the emergence of postindustrial or
postcapitalist or post-Fordist economies, as well as postmodern societies
and cultures. As academic disciplines, we are in the process of
considering whether or not it is worthwhile to devote substantial
resources to the analysis of "postindustrial" or "postmodern" systems.

To the point, the verdict is open. Social theory in France has been
most vigorous in advancing the case for a qualitative rupture in the
fabric of complex systems. The "poststructuralists" — Baudrillard,
Derrida, Foucault, and Lyotard have each, in their own way, argued that
we are experiencing and observing fundamental alterations in economic
and cultural affairs (Poster, 1990). While these perspectives are
increasingly influential in English and U.S. academic circles, enthusiasm
is far from overwhelming. Questions have been raised the centrality of
these changes (Are we really looking at major changes, or are they
restricted to one [minor] segment of the system?) as well as the
intellectual and political agendas of the new theorists (Are they really
promoting a conservative quietism though the relevant to community or

microlevel processes?.

An equally important question, in terms of the professions, particularly librarianship, concerns the emphasis one puts on economic and cultural issues within debates about postindustrialism and postmodernism. To what extent are we facing problems related to the economic processes — the creation of an information economy — and to what degree are we looking at more purely cultural phenomena — the growth of postmodern culture? In a more Marxian form, we can ask whether we are looking at the emergence of a new mode of production or, as Mark Poster (1990) suggests, a new "mode of communication." If the changes are primarily economic, then professions may look to jurisdictional strategies that focus on labour market positions, and maximizing one's place there. Alternatively, cultural concerns suggest a reexamination of the intellectual bases of the profession's credibility, and a concomitant examination of the sociolinguistic foundations of acceptable new claims for professional jurisdiction.

The research we have conducted for this project indicates that the magnitude of change in a postindustrial or postmodern direction that can be successfully captured by the library profession is quite small. Library work has changed somewhat, particularly in the area of special libraries; there has been a small degree of overlap in the intellectual endeavours of library and information science; and there has been institutional innovation in medical, scientific, and technical areas that parallels these shifts.

While there are some modest indications of new jurisdictions to be competed for, librarianship has not made appreciable inroads in these new domains in terms of job placements. Further, various combinations and permutations in the curricula of library and information schools provide less evidence of competitive success than regional adaptations to opportunities in the Canadian political economy.[1] The data we have collected also suggest that current social changes have not altered the work of the profession in any profound way. There are indications, both in our work survey in chapter 2 and our curriculum analysis in chapter 7, that both new computer and telecommunication technologies have modified the way librarianship is taught and conducted. Nevertheless, the qualitative interviews suggest that much of the successful incorporation of new technology has been pragmatic, with little impact on other work areas or on conceptions of the profession.

Basic Patterns

Our research facilitates a reasonably broad assessment of the current status and possible futures of Canadian librarianship. While it is not wise to extrapolate directly from existing conditions to an indefinite future, knowledge of current circumstances should give indications, at different levels, of possible trends, as well as the prospect of trends leading to cumulative effects.

Our survey analysis of current work conditions lends little support to the basic propositions that come from the information paradigm about library work and libraries as institutions. While there is a considerable amount of agreement across different library settings, Canadian librarians distinguish strongly among these various settings in terms of the probable changes that information technologies will bring, with special libraries remaining the focus of these changes. Further, when public, school, and academic librarians do anticipate technological change in their areas, it is predominantly with a view to improving the quality of traditional services, especially in a period of economic constraint. Again, while there is a perception that all librarians will have to improve their abilities to work with new computer and other electronic technologies, current effort devoted to such work is limited in many settings, and these skills require small amounts of time to learn.

What emerges from our survey is a picture of Canadian librarianship in which the structure of library settings remains clearly distinct, with a major bifurcation between public, school and academic libraries on one side, and public and private special libraries on the other. These differences in settings are reflected in the work experiences of their librarians, and are associated with the very different interpretations that Canadian librarians bring to the changing nature of their work. In other words, the information paradigm is much more appropriate to the analysis of special libraries, and has limited applicability to the more traditional library world that is organized around a public service ethic.

Our comparative analysis of activities at the National Library of Canada and CISTI demonstrates that there is some differentiation in the nature and substance of information being handled by the two institutions. The National Library has a general subject range that is limited to Canadian materials, while CISTI concentrates on medical, technical, and scientific information with a broader geographic audience. In a similar fashion, the National Library only utilizes bibliographic databases, while CISTI has somewhat more diversified databases.

Nevertheless, these two central Canadian institutions are both predominantly libraries, and have more salient commonalities than differences.

Our examination of relevant professional literature provides little indication that we are observing an intellectual convergence in library science and information science. There has been some overlap spanning a two-decade period that is concerned primarily with the practicalities of utilizing new communications and computer technologies in different work spheres. However, we still have professional literature that is closely tied to the type of science being considered.

Our earlier studies of labour market conditions generated results that are also suggestive of segmented labour markets, with alternatives to traditional institutional markets generating little demand for graduates of existing MLIS programs. In chapter 5, our analysis of jobs in Canada's "emerging information market" proved that both the jobs and required skills in the new market are quite specific. Information systems managers are expected to have a substantial package of computer-related skills, while public relations and communications personnel, records managers, and research analysts are required to have data organization and retrieval skills. M.L.I.S. credentials or skills are in little demand for such positions.

In chapter 6, we estimate that fewer than 15 percent of MLIS graduates have found employment outside conventional settings in the first five years of their careers. Further, as only one-quarter of the jobs in nonconventional establishments can be considered part of an emerging information market, our analysis indicates that less than 4 percent of jobs obtained are ones opening new doors for MLIS graduates.[2] Finally, the alternative sources of employment made only minor issue of the skills acquired in MLIS programs. While Canadian MLIS programs have all made moves to incorporate information science in their curriculum, our scrutiny of these programs suggests substantial regional variations in the extent to which information science has been introduced. Our study also suggests differing regional and institutional mandates that may make successful reform of these professional programs tricky. It is obvious that each unit will have to work out its own accommodations for new computer technologies. The problem remains how one balances this new emphasis with standard expectations in the selection, acquisition, and organization of text-based information activities.

What each of our empirical chapters indicates, in different ways, are the difficulties in crossing professional boundaries successfully.

Whether one is looking at professional work, professional literature, labour market conditions, or professional education, one is simultaneously impressed by the persistence of traditional categories, and the dangers inherent in altering them. However, it is also clear that change is coming, and the question becomes one of negotiating transitions without jeopardizing the integrity of a professional identity.

Qui Bono?*

Despite a divergence between the advocates of the Information paradigm and those who adhere to the Service paradigm, and despite evidence that the identification of librarianship with "information" is not an accurate depiction of the reality of the profession, the Information paradigm has acquired obvious popularity among a substantial segment of librarians.

As could have been expected, the Information paradigm finds its greatest support from among the ranks of those librarians who are working in information centers and corporate special libraries. These individuals are often compelled to upgrade their image in order to obtain professional status within their organizations, a status to which a false "clerical" image of librarians is an obstacle.

Another source of support for the Information paradigm comes because of career considerations among younger librarians. Since the 1960s there has taken place a substantial change in the type of recruits coming into the profession. Today they are mostly career-oriented and highly-motivated individuals who are displacing the bookish introverts of the past "sensible shoes" variety. They chafe at the negative image, status, and mobility constraints that have until now characterized librarians. For them, the substitution of the label "professional information manager" has a particularly strong appeal, and they tend to be attracted by a more "relevant" image. As Louis Vagianos phrased it some years ago,

> It appears that the "today" people of the profession feel
> the term (librarian) is pejorative — that it is too fussy,
> dusty, musty, rusty and crusty, suggestive of pallid

---

* This section was written by Boris Raymond.

eunuchs and prunish reclusives.

How can we create a new term around which all can
rally? This new term should deal with the collection,
storage and distribution of data and must satisfy three
basic criteria:
1) it should help every practitioner make more money;
2) it should increase every practitioner's prestige;
    (and),
3) ...if what we are and what we do is not as
    important as who the public thinks we are and
    what the public thinks we do, then clearly, a
    "quantum" jump in our social prestige and the
    monies we are paid could be just around the
    corner (1972a: 2701).

Attempts to modify the popular perception of the library profession
quite naturally turn toward associating it with advanced technology, a
field that commands both higher prestige and greater financial rewards.
The concept of a "professional information manager" accomplishes just
that.

Librarians are understandably enthusiastic about any
proposition that implies an enhanced role for their
profession.   Their enthusiasm for the idea of an
information society is so extensive that there is little
questioning of the proposition among them. (Birdsall,
1994: 16)

Another reason for the current tropism towards "information" is that
the word caters to the "techies," those individuals in our ranks who
would rather deal with something concrete than with intellectual
abstractions. These people would far rather surf on Internet than provide
educational and intellectual service to their clientele (Roma Harris,
1992). The additional bonus of the term "information" for them is that
the term is a link to the wonders of computer technology, to those who
consider reading a text in a print-on-paper format to be an antediluvian
practice. In the words of Susanna L. Davidsen, technology librarian and
operations manager, MLink (CRISTAL, October 9, 1995): "It ain"t
about books, it"s about information."

A major boost for the "information manager" concept is its promise of liberation from the "clerical" mentality that has too often prevailed among librarians in the past. The impact of the new electronic technologies has expanded the number and efficacy of library functions (MARC, the creation of bibliographic utilities, the expansion of search capacity of databases, and the speeding up of global communications for such library functions as interlibrary lending). In many areas such technology has eliminated the need for the meticulous busywork so essential in the past. Association with these remarkable technologies has undoubtedly served to glamorize the hitherto low image of librarians.

Another major source of support for the Information paradigm comes from the LIS sector of the profession. By the late 1970s, a significant drop had occurred in the growth rate of the library employment market; public libraries, school libraries, and academic libraries were no longer expanding, and the demand for new librarians decreased drastically. In addition, improvement of library salaries discouraged job turnover, as did more generous maternity leaves. Taken together with a substantial loss of professional library positions due to the de-skilling impact of computer technology, these phenomena resulted in a surplus of newly graduated librarians relative to job openings. Coming as it did at a time when the number of MLIS graduates was the highest in history, these developments placed many LIS schools in a position of either closing or attempting to find a new employment market for their graduates. One such source was found in a hypothesized "emerging information market."

In the present climate of financial constraint, university administrations are being forced to cut their budgets and to eliminate academic units. Those library schools that did not succeed in establishing for themselves a clearly identifiable theoretical spectrum found themselves somewhat more vulnerable to closure. They quite naturally attempted to demonstrate a theoretical foundation for their discipline. One of the most effective ways of accomplishing this was by incorporating the term "information," and identifying their discipline with "information science." In such a way they were able to obtain the necessary protective coloration to maintain their program, even if the curricula changes often amount to little more than the addition of the term "information" and some computer literacy courses to traditional library instruction.[3]

At the same time, because enrollment in the information management stream in almost all MLIS schools is not sufficient to support an academic program, there existed a very strong pressure on these schools not to "go the separate route," but rather to create an appearance of "convergence" between the traditional library curriculae and the "innovative information management" stream. Such a marriage of convenience, however, was often accomplished only at the cost of eliminating the "library" designation from their programs.

A further contributing factor to the rise of the Information paradigm was the implementation of a national- and state-level economic austerity that aimed at reducing the tax-supported free public libraries, and transferring as much of their work as possible to for-profit business and industry "information centers." In fact, it is arguable that the acceptance of a forced integration of librarianship and the "information management" will result in the destruction of general librarianship as we know it.

The Debate Intensifies

The controversy about the long-term applicability of the information paradigm has been sharpened by a diversity of responses from intellectual and professional opponents. In the past several years, individuals who value the service traditions particularly associated with school and public libraries, as well as contemporary feminists who view these traditions as gendered ones, have been constructing alternative visions of the future. These endeavours have been complemented by statements from inside the profession that raise doubts about the nature and depth of the transition to an information economy and to an information-based profession.

The first type of response is typified by Michael Harris and Stan Hannah's new study, *Into the Future: The Foundations of Library and Information Services in the Post-Industrial Era*. In a thorough reexamination of American theories of postindustrialism, Harris and Hannah (1994) provide a persuasive critique of Daniel Bell's original formulation about the coming of a postindustrial society, as well as Frederick W. Lancaster's extrapolations of Bell's ideas into the area of an information profession that would emerge from the change to a "paperless" society. In each case, general and specific, Harris and Hannah identify unwarranted elements of technological determinism, as well as strategic ambiguities that permit professional readers to locate paths to a secure niche in the new information economy. Both Bell and

Lancaster overestimate the prospects for a new class of information professionals to assume new power and prestige in postindustrial systems because their faith in scientific transformations downplays the political and cultural constraints on economic change. Lancaster is criticized for misunderstanding the degree to which "the librarian's cherished role as a neutral servant of democracy" is connected to "the fact that the library was deliberately privileged by the profession in service of its mission to protect free and equitable access to information in a democratic republic." (Harris and Hannah, 1994: 47, 49)

Using a political economy framework, Harris and Hannah then propose an alternative "periodization" of the era following the second world war. In theoretical terms, librarianship has been affected by a cyclical shift involving, in James O'Connor's terms, a move from "legitimation" in the Kennedy regime to one of "accumulation" in the Bush and Reagan years. At an institutional level, the years from the mid-1960s forward saw the American library system generously funded with resources for books, periodicals, new buildings, and augmented training for librarians. However, these resources were contingent on libraries and librarians agreeing to act as a conduit for high culture in society at large. In Harris and Hannah's terms, "From the mid 1960s, the library's structural and functional characteristics were determined by its definition as an institution contrived to consume, preserve, transmit, and reproduce high culture in printed form as a public good" (1994:70). By contrast, the last fifteen years of American history have been an era of retrenchment, a time in which the "accumulation" concerns of the American state have led to cutbacks and a search for ways to introduce market forces into the cultural domain. Harris and Hannah are impressed by the extent to which the new accumulation agenda has reshaped both American cultural activities and library systems. Specifically, they argue that librarians interested in preserving the "general normative consensus" that "existed from the late 1940s to the 1970s" appear to be "incapable of acknowledging the extent to which the idea of information as a public good in American society has been discredited or completely abandoned" (1994: 139, 142).

This political economy of information and librarianship leads Harris and Hannah to reexamine the nature of work and professionalism in contemporary librarianship. They believe that information technology, understood as a combination of computer hardware and software as well as associated telecommunications capacities, is modifying the nature of work in libraries. However, the changes are going to occur slowly, and they can be usefully integrated into the library as a workplace. Too many of the existing library automation projects have been mechanically introduced, with insufficient appreciation of the peculiarities of library work. For example, many OPAC (online public access catalog) systems are inefficient because simple attempts to replicate the traditional card catalog have resulted in limited numbers of access points (1994: 125-127). This form of adaptation leaves many users with a high rate of failure in subject searches.

Further, the appropriate introduction of information technology may undermine the traditional bureaucratic forms of control characteristic of library work precisely because hierarchy is, in this new setting, inefficient and unprofitable. However, the future, if it is to be a democratic one, must break with the elitist versions of contemporary liberalism. It is not a question of bringing high culture to the masses for their betterment, but rather one of meeting the requirements of ordinary citizens searching to improve their social and economic status. The exclusive focus of traditional liberalism on abstract intellectual freedoms must expand to create "access to the intelligence" necessary for socioeconomic betterment (1994: 100).

In keeping with trends in contemporary feminist thought, Roma Harris has constructed an analysis of postindustrial trends that emphasizes the gendered aspects of librarianship that have the prospect of forestalling any direct transition to an information profession. In *Librarianship: The Erosion of a Woman's Profession* (1992), Harris proposes that librarianship, like nursing, teaching and social work, is preeminently a woman's profession that has a "democratic" or "nonpaternalistic type of service orientation," as opposed to the managerial and technological orientations of the higher-status male professions (1992: 15, 19-20). The more democratic service traditions of women's professions have the potential to resist misdirected attempts to transform librarianship into a group in search of professional elevation through the incorporation of information technology and its associated scientific theorizing.

However, if the feminist project is to be successful, it must appreciate the sources of its past and current difficulties. First, Harris argues that explanations of professional culture that have concentrated on the gender composition of occupations have typically made the mistake of accepting sex role stereotypes ("genteel traditionalism, ineffectual males and shushing spinsters" [72]) as integral, rather than accidental, characteristics of librarianship. Alternatively, if one begins by examining the degree to which women have been recruited into librarianship to staff bureaucracies that need subordinates, stereotypes, as well as other negative cultural assessments, can be better comprehended as forms of social control. With this understanding, women in the professions will be better able to resist attempts to downgrade their work through "territorial encroachment" from established professions, "deskilling," and the creation of two-tier credentials (e.g., bachelor of social work versus master of social work). Further, a structural analysis will help one better appreciate the real limits of "image management" as a method of self-advancement. Women need to look at using their unions and professional associations more effectively, and they also would benefit from building connections outside their particular professions.

The complementary academic challenges provided by Michael Harris and Stan Hannah, and Roma Harris, have the salutary effect of broadening the debate about the past and future of librarianship. Starting from somewhat different theoretical benchmarks, they alert us to implicit historical flaws in postindustrial theorizing, as well as explicit problems with the empirical accuracy of postindustrial expectations. However, both accounts have a tendency to blur the inevitable overlap of elite and populist strands in the democratic commitments of librarianship in the United States, and to underestimate the difficulties in implementing a more populist vision. Further, these analyses do not distinguish clearly enough among different types of libraries (public, school, university, special), or speak directly enough to the question of "nontraditional" work. Many of the conflicts they have identified are associated with the varying demands of these alternative work settings, and one can only appreciate the persistence and significance of the debate by taking these differences into account.

In *The Myth of the Electronic Library*, William Birdsall uses his extensive career experiences as a university librarians and administrator to analyze the two leading perspectives on libraries and librarianship in North America.[4] The myth of the "electronic library," a product of technological developments over the last twenty-five years, is challenging the older "library as place" myth for dominance in our understanding of the nature of libraries and librarianship. The myth of the "electronic library" has an associated rhetoric of the "library without walls," the "global village library," where rapid access to information for dependent clients becomes a unique focus with "intermediary librarians" facilitating passage on the electronic highway. This myth, which as an institutional base in special and academic libraries as well as the scientific research community, is to some degree supplanting the late-nineteenth-century myth of the "library as place," the tradition of public libraries, both in small communities and larger urban centers. The public library represents a source of stability and personal attachment in a rapidly changing world that frequently is "lacking any coherence" (1994: 65). Citizens have developed emotional ties to these public institutions, places in which librarians, as personal service professionals, foster individualism and self-sufficiency among library users.

Birdsall's volume is particularly good at identifying deeper flaws in the "electronic library" myth. He first demonstrates that the "utopian meta-myth of the electronic revolution," and its related theories of a postindustrial, information society, have encountered significant empirical hurdles in the dramatically reduced growth of information sectors and information occupations in the North American economy. Second, he persuasively argues that the history of the professions in the twentieth century, even for traditional professions like medicine, is a history of bureaucratization. Librarianship, as one of a number of personal service professions, is intimately related to the expansion of public bureaucracies. More important, the increasing cost, and operating expenses associated with modern technologies make professionals of all sorts more reliant on bureaucracies. Drawing on his own experience in developing an interuniversity consortium that owns and operates an on-line, integrated library system, Birdsall concludes that "if we can look forward to the electronic librarian and the electronic library, be prepared for the electronic bureaucracy as well" (1994: 96).

Birdsall's conclusion that librarianship can create a new myth that will bridge the two dominant ones, and thus preserve notions of community and individualism simultaneously, is less persuasive. It may be true that libraries can benefit from postmodern architecture (e.g., he new Chicago Public Library) and sensibilities (the "sensuous library," the "therapeutic librarian"). Nevertheless, the prospect for a genuine synthesis seems less likely than a continuation of the "profound ambiguity" that characterizes the current situation. The diverse institutional bases of the competing myths are unlikely to facilitate such integration, nor are their representatives likely to contribute directly to such a project.

At a more specific level, Walt Crawford and Michael Gorman have raised major questions about the practical advances that librarianship of any sort can make with electronic communications. In a book that is provocatively entitled *Future Libraries: Dreams, Madness and Reality*, Crawford and Gorman explore the psychological and economic limitations of electronic media as new tools available for the "advancement of knowledge and preservation of culture" (1995: 3). The authors persuasively argue that when one is dealing with linear text of more than a few paragraphs, books retain their superiority to electronic alternatives for both psychological and economic reasons. At a psychological level, books remain an "appropriate technology" because electronic displays (1) tire you by shining light in your face as you read; (2) typically provide less precision in the resolution of textual materials; and (3) generally slow reading speed, as well as comprehension, due to the smaller areas that can be examined (1995: 19-22). In a parallel fashion, reasonable economic estimates make it clear that print is still the preferred vehicle for short-run monographs and journals, trade and medium-run books, and particularly mass-market paperbacks. To date, only short-lived reference works appear to be better delivered via electronic distribution (1995: 26-30). However, when one moves to CD-ROMs, one is not making appreciable progress toward the virtual library because "CD-ROMs are, fundamentally, just big, hard-to-read but easy-to-search texts in little packages; they are published items that libraries buy and house, and to which they provide access" (1995: 27). Further, many of the comparisons that have favorably evaluated new electronic alternatives tend to ignore "secondary costs of electronic distribution." Not only do "online resources require terminals or workstations" and "CD-ROM publications require computers and, increasingly, networking," it is also probable that our "global rat's nest," the Internet, and other electronic networks will start charging fees, in many cases commercial ones, for access (1995: 27, 77, 99, 102).

According to Crawford and Gorman, the basic mistake made by futurists is the assumption that there is a rather easy, low-cost transition from invention to practical utilization. In fact, most innovations fail, and the typical experience with new technologies is adaptation, then displacement (1995: 43-50). The probable failure of on-line texts, such as Project Gutenberg, and the seemingly intractable difficulties with the widespread use of electronic journals are two systematic examples of the difficulties new electronic projects are encountering (1995: 59-61, 65-68). Crawford and Gorman propose, by way of response, that all contemporary libraries involve a mix of services and means of communication that transcend the false dichotomy of electronic versus non-electronic media. The future library will include "both print and electronic communication, "both linear text and hyptertext," "both mediation by librarians and direct access," "both collections and access," and "both edifice and interface" (1995: 9-10, 180-181).

While Crawford and Gorman are very effective in many of their specific empirical evaluations and economic assessments, their "modernist" faith in libraries as entities that contribute to growth and progress through "the conquest of space and time" (1995: 9) probably leads them to use strident rhetoric to characterize opposing views. Terms like "technovandals," "new barbarians," and "electronic beach bums" (1995: 36, 83, 105, 116) not only demean alternatives, they trivialize what is a serious intellectual debate. Like many of their opponents, Crawford and Gorman are prepared to concede little by way of genuine diversity to different institutional forms. While they do characterize public and academic libraries in detail (1995: 133-149), they are not prepared to acknowledge that special libraries may be very different settings, not merely variations on a theme. It is possible that what unites libraries is not, in some cases, as important as the distinctions.

The Struggle for Professional Jurisdiction

The academic and professional debate about competing paradigms intersects with conflict among various interest groups in the library and information domain. At a sociological level, one can conceptualize the paradigms being discussed in this book as "professional ideologies" that are being utilized by particular individuals and groups to establish professional claims and to shape an uncertain future. If one follows Andrew Abbott (1988) in emphasizing the work dimensions of library and information science, as we have done above, then the primary focus of analysis here shifts to the question of connections between professional group boundaries and the control of work. In terms of the typology introduced in the second chapter, one can then argue that our competing paradigms are roughly aligned with specific categories of library work. As suggested in chapter 2, the information paradigm is associated with the work of special libraries, while the Library Service paradigm is connected to work in public, school, and academic libraries.

The initial appeal of the information paradigm as a new formulation in the 1960s and 1970s was tied to the prospect that new job markets and opportunities would emerge as the information economy expanded. The new postindustrial order, and particularly the private sector, would create new work settings that required increased competence in computer technologies and telecommunications. These new jobs, in turn, would augment the professional status of librarianship because they would add higher paying positions to the occupational mix. The additional possibility of interacting with higher status clients would, by reflection, increase the status of the profession, as well as the influence it would have in public affairs.[5]

While new visions are easier to accommodate in an expansionary economy, the information paradigm did manage to generate some unrest, even in this earlier period, because it implied a reorganization of priorities, both intellectual and professional. The universalistic terms in which the arguments about a "paperless" society were formulated not only attempted to legitimize the expansion of what were minority interests, but they also challenged the practical intellectual basis on which traditional librarianship rests. In other words, the professional jurisdiction was not only expanding, but it was changing. Minimally, traditional professional niches would have to be modified; as likely, they would have to be partially abandoned.[6]

When one relocates this kind of conflict in the worsening economic circumstances in the mid-1970s and beyond, the possibility for accommodations within the profession diminish. Not only were other higher status professions, like computing science, engineering, and management studies, beginning to respond to potential incursion on their domains, but the worsening prospects for new entrants to the profession intensified debates about appropriate professional education. If traditional employment in public libraries was diminishing, the evident lack of success in ostensible new markets increased the pressure to reevaluate competing definitions of professional jurisdiction.

To survive, even on a temporary basis, professions must demonstrate the capacity to apply abstract knowledge effectively to real cases. To date, the promise of a new "information science" (Schrader, 1986) has not coalesced as a unified body of abstract knowledge that can establish a stable jurisdiction for "library and information science."[7] The simultaneous downturn of traditional job markets confronts the existing profession with unpalatable alternatives. One can scale down one's ambitions, and the magnitude of one's professional group, to accommodate contemporary circumstances, albeit with some necessary modification demanded by new technologies. On the other hand, one can continue working toward a new, unified science, and perhaps anticipate an upturn in the private sector. Whichever path one takes, there are major risks involved. The heightened stakes involved in strategic errors at this point have undoubtedly fueled the increasing stridency of the debate about the future of a profession.

Notes

1. To be fair, one must acknowledge that some of the effects we are searching for have been diminished by the current recession. While it is difficult to disentangle professional trajectories form business cycle effects, there seems to be little reason for optimism about the impact of an economic recovery on the amount or pace of professional change.

2. More recent data for five of the seven Canadian M.L.I.S. schools (excluding UBC and Montreal) show that the patterns we have identified both in terms of alternative employment and "emerging information market" jobs remained relatively similar in 1992. (Correspondence from Jean Tague-Sutcliffe, dean, Graduate School of Library and Information Science, The University of Western Ontario, September 8, 1993). The proportion of placement positions for 1992 graduates in emerging information jobs was 5.4 percent (two people in the "computer industry," twelve as "consultant/brokers," two in the "information industry," and three in "records management," out of a total of 164).

3. If the schools had "information science" in their names, it wouldn"t have been so easy for the administrators to use the "libraries are passe" excuse. (Arlene Taylor, CRISTAL, November 30, 1994).

4. These comments are based on an earlier review of the work (Apostle, 1995).

5. An important corollary of these arguments, as discussed above, is the proposition that work in public, school, and academic settings would also be modified and upgraded by new technologies.

6. These changes, it was widely feared, would also be accompanied by increased internal stratification within the profession. Not only would the status differences among clients increase (from children to business people), but there would be a degradation in the skills required by an increasing number of people doing library work. Abbott (1988: 145) argues that the short-run impact of computerization on professions may be negative, but the overall impact of technological innovation, both direct and indirect, is positive (1988: 146).

7. As Schrader points out, the connection between information science and library science has received little attention. Schrader argues that "nowhere is weak conceptualization in the definitional literature of information science more apparent than in the treatment of the domain of library science. Typically, there is no reference to it at all, not even a denial of its one-hundred-year-old literature. At best, the references are superficial and incomplete. Efforts to tear apart the disciplinary domains have been consistently inadequate" (1986: 200).

APPENDIX A

SAMPLE DESIGN AND METHODOLOGY
FOR CHAPTER 2

Our survey was conducted as a stratified cluster sample of all professional librarians in Canada. The population was stratified both by library type and region, with clusters being drawn on the basis of library size (number of professional librarians employed) within the twenty library type/region categories. Given the subject matter of the survey, we expected significant variation by library type. Our experience with other surveys, particularly ones dealing with library employment, convinced us to include region as a stratifying dimension. Our estimates of the population, and the total sample drawn, are given in table A.1.

TABLE A.1. SAMPLE/POPULATION ESTIMATES FOR
PROFESSIONAL LIBRARIANS IN CANADA BY REGIONAL
AND LIBRARY TYPE

Region	Public	School	Academic	Special	Total
Atlantic (New-foundland, New Brunswick, Nova Scotia, Prince Edward Island)	23/180	3/23	23/170	12/96	61/469
Quebec	58/399	3/19	93/688	25/190	179/1296
Ontario	171/1223	40/295	133/901	110/788	454/3207

Table A.1. — <u>continued</u>

Prairies (Alberta, Manitoba, Saskatchewan, Northwest Territories)	59/376	12/85	74/498	38/214	183/ 1173
British Columbia (Yukon)	39/271	11/75	44/292	18/120	112/ 758
Total	350/2449	69/497	367/ 2549	203/ 1408	989/ 6903

Our fieldwork was conducted by the Survey Centre at the Gorsebrook Research Institute, Saint Mary's University.

The Survey Centre, established in 1986 under the auspices of the Gorsebrook Research Institute, is a "project consistent with the Institute's mandate to provide research support to scholars in the region. The rationale for creating a survey support service came from the Institute's own research needs, i.e. the Donner/SSHRC funded Land and Sea Project, as well as the general perception that such a service would greatly enhance the survey research capacity of scholars in the region. The Centre, a not-for-profit organization, has been financially self sufficient since 1988. It receives no monetary support from either the University or the Gorsebrook Research Institute. Contracts are negotiated on a fee-for-service basis. In addition, the Centre provides a considerable amount of pro bono assistance, particularly in the preparation of funding applications."

Our completed surveys are distributed as shown in table A.2. Proportionately, our response rates are higher for special libraries and lower for academic libraries. In the first two instances, the relevance of the study is fairly apparent. In the case of academic libraries, we think we run into organizational problems in the distribution of questionnaires for relatively large clusters. More specifically, the work involved in arranging distribution, even with our offers of direct assistance, created difficulties. It should be also noted that our completion rates have been affected by the current economic climate. One major university library, which had experienced a 20 percent cut back in staff, and with the prospect of more cuts coming, felt it would be too threatening to ask its staff to participate in the study. Another major public library encountered union opposition to the distribution of a detailed questionnaire about current work responsibilities. These two institutions accounted for seventeen potential interviews.

TABLE A.2. SURVEY RETURNS BY
REGION AND LIBRARY TYPE

Library Type					
Region	Public	School	Academic	Special	Total
Atlantic (Newfound-land, New Brunswick, Nova Scotia, Prince Edward Island)	15/23	2/3	15/23	11/12	43/61
Quebec	23/58	1/3	45/93	21/25	90/179
Ontario	88/171	25/40	46/133	80/110	239/454
Prairies (Alberta, Manitoba, Saskatchewan, Northwest Territories)	42/59	7/12	32/74	22/38	103/183
British Columbia (Yukon)	41/39	6/11	25/44	8/18	80/112
Total	209/350	41/69	163/367	142/203	555/989

A more detailed methodological discussion of the survey is available on request from the authors.

APPENDIX B

SAMPLE DESIGN AND METHODOLOGY FOR CHAPTER 3

As preliminary step, population estimates for the total number of articles in a journal series (period 1971-1991 inclusive) were obtained for each journal in the following manner:

1. The total number of issues for each journal series was obtained by multiplying the number of issues per year by the total number of years in the study period of 1971-1991.
2. Once the total number of issues was calculated for a journal, 10 per cent of that total was taken. For example, if a journal had one hundred issues, ten issues were selected for estimating the total number of articles appearing over the course of a journal series.
3. This number was then divided into the total number of issues to provide a sampling interval period that covers the time period of the journal.
4. A starting point was randomly generated.
5. Commencing with the starting issue and every "nth" issue, after the total number of articles was counted from each journal selected.
6. The number of articles was totaled for each sample of journals and multiplied by the total number of issues divided by the number of sample journals. This yielded an estimate of the total number of articles appearing over the course of a journal series.

For example, the Canadian Library Journal had 11 issues out of a total of 126 issues selected for an article count. The sample yielded a total of 73 articles. Population estimates were obtained by:

73 Articles x (126 Issues/11 Sample Issues) = 836 Articles

Forty articles were selected in a systematic fashion from each journal series commencing with a randomly generated start point. The sampling interval was calculated by dividing the number of articles to be selected (forty in each case) into the total number of article population estimates for each journal. For example, the Canadian Library Journal yielded a sampling interval of 21 (836/40 = 20.9). In this instance, every twenty-first article was selected.

Population Estimates

Library Journals   Number of Articles

1. *Canadian Library Journal*   836
2. *Library Quarterly*   237
3. *Library Trends*   779
4. *Library Journal (American)*   1684
5. *Wilson Library Bulletin*   1008
6. *Library Resources and Technical Services*   618
7. *British Library Journal*   168
Total Population Estimate   5330

Information Sciences

1. *Canadian Journal of Information Services*   205
2. *Journal of American Society for
   Information Science (JASIS)*   893
3. *Information Technology and Libraries*   496
4. *Information Processing and Management*   878
5. *American Society for Information Sciences -
   Proceedings (ASIS)*   1522
6. *Education for Information*   145
7. *Information Scientist*   504
Total Population Estimate   4643

APPENDIX C

CLASSIFICATION OF ACTIVITIES SUBSUMED UNDER "INFORMATION WORK"

A classification of the activities subsumed under "information work," was provided by a British researcher, Nick Moore (1989: 46-47). This study classified the emerging information market into ten fields.

1. Library work, or jobs involving library as opposed to information skills and based within a unit described as a library.
2. Information work, or jobs requiring the traditional skills of an information worker and usually based within an information unit or service.
3. Research and information, or posts that, in addition to information work, require a substantial element of research work involving collection of data from nondocumentary sources.
4. Information technology, or posts that were primarily concerned with the use and application of information technology.
5. Indexing and abstracting. Most posts in these groups were concerned quite simply with indexing and abstracting. Some, however, also included an element of technical writing.
6. Servicing the information industry. This group consists of posts with firms and organizations that service the information industry, and libraries, such as bibliographical database suppliers and library automation services.
7. Advice work. This category does not really have an equivalent in North America.
8. Public relations, when these jobs are described as those of an "information officer."
9. Management information. Posts in this group were primarily concerned with providing information about internal operations to its management for use in decision making
10. Records management. Posts in this group are primarily concerned with the organization, storage, and retrieval of files and other documentary records that are related to the work of an organization.

BIBLIOGRAPHY

Abbott, Andrew. *The System of Professions: An Essay on the Division of Expert Labor.* Chicago: the University of Chicago Press, 1988.

ALA Special Committee on Library School Closings. *Report.* Assistant Vice Chancellor for Library and Information Services Planning, University of California at Los Angeles, Los Angeles, California, 1991.

American Library Directory 1994-95. New Providence, N.J.: R. R. Bowker, 1995.

Anderson, Lynne. *Exploring Careers in Library Science.* New York: Rosen Publishing Group, 1985.

Apostle, Richard. "Review of the Myth of the Electronic Library," *The Canadian Journal of Information and Library Science* 20 (1995): 54-55.

_____, and Boris Raymond. "Librarianship and the Information Paradigm," *Canadian Library Journal* 43 (1986): 377-384.

_____, Boris Raymond, and Paul Smith. "The Impact of Computer Technology on the Library Profession," *APLA Bulletin* 48 (1984): 6-7.

Bell, Daniel. *The Coming of Post-Industrial Society: A Venture in Social Forecasting.* New York: Basic Books, 1973.

Berry, John. "Editorial: Confronting Cronin's Complaint," *Library Journal* 120, no. 15 (March 15, 1995): 6.

Birdsall, William. *The Myth of the Electronic Library: Librarianship and Social Change in America.* Westport, Conn.: Greenwood Press, 1994.

Boorstin, Daniel. "Gresham's Law: Knowledge or Information," *Antiquarian Bookman* 69 (1982):1379-1388.

Borgman, Christine, and Jorge Schement. "Information Science and Communication Research," in Michael Pemberton and Ann Prentice eds., *Information Science: The Interdisciplinary Context.* New York: Neal-Schuman Publishers, 1990.

Brown, Jack. "Resources and Services of the National Science Library (Excerpt from His Annual Report 1967-1968)," *Ontario Library Review*, 53 (March 1969): 2-10.

Buckland, Michael. *Information and Information Systems.* New York: Greenwood Press, 1991.

Bullock, Bonnie, Mary VanBuskirk, and Margaret Walshe. "The Training Requirements for Version II of CAN/OLE," *The Canadian Journal of Information Science* 12 (1987): 132-138.

"Canada Institute for Scientific and Technical Information," *Ontario Library Review* 59 (1994): 126.

Canadian Institute for Scientific and Technical Information. "CISTI: A Plan for the Future," Ottawa: National Research Council Canada, 1992.

_____. "Mission Statement," Ottawa: National Research Council Canada, 1990.

Chen, Ching-Chih. "Multimedia Information Delivery: The Challenge to Librarians in the Visual Information Age," in *Electronic Library Linking People, Information, and Technology.* Chicago: Reference and Adult Services Division American Library Association, RASD Occasional Papers 14, 1992, pp. 3-9.

Chen, Ching-Chih, Susan Raskin, and Diane Tebbetts. "Products of Graduate Library and Information Science Schools: Untapped Resources?" *Education for Information*, 2 (1984): 163-190.

CISTI News. "CISTI Services at a Glance," Ottawa, National Research Council Canada 12 (September 1994e): 8.

_____. "Question Box. Does CISTI Collect only Canadian Sci/Tech Information? Ottawa National Research Council Canada 12 (September 1994d): 7.

_____. "Romulus Receives Award," Ottawa National Research Council Canada 12 (September 1994c): 7.

_____. "Research Journals 65 Years Later," Ottawa, National Research Council Canada 12 (September 1994b): 3.

_____. "Announcing the New 'Reference Plus' Service," Ottawa, National Research Council Canada 12 (June 1994a): 1.

_____. "From Dreams to Reality," Ottawa, National Research Council Canada, Anniversary Issue (1984b): 8-9.

_____. "CISTI's Roots and Branches An Historical Survey," Ottawa, National Research Council Canada, Anniversary Issue (1984a): 2-8.

Crawford, Susan. "The Origin and Development of a Concept: The Information Society," *Bulletin of the Medical Library Association*, 71 (1983): 380-385.

Crawford, Walt, and Michael Gorman. *Future Libraries: Dreams, Madness and Reality.* Chicago: American Library Association, 1995.

Cronin, Blaise. "Nichemanship for the Nineties," *Education for Information*, 5 (1987): 321-325.

Dafoe, Elizabeth. "A National Library of Canada," *Canadian Library Association Bulletin* (1948): 14-17.

Daniel, Evelyn. "New Curriculum Areas," pp. 53-70 in Richard Gardner, ed., *Education of Library and Information Professionals.* Littleton, Colorado: Libraries Unlimited, 1987.

_____. "The Library/Information School in Context: The Place of Library Information Science Education within Higher

Education," *Library Trends* 35 (1986): 623-643.

Debons, Anthony, Donald King, Una Mansfield, and Donald Shirey. *The Information Professional: Survey of an Emerging Field.* New York: Marcel Dekker, 1981.

Directory of Libraries in Canada. Toronto: Micromedia, 1994.

Donnelly, F. Dolores. "The National Library of Canada. A Historical Analysis of the Forces which Contributed to its Establishment and to the Identification of its Role and Responsibilities." Ottawa: Canadian Library Association, 1973.

Duffy, Jack, Boris Raymond, and Richard Apostle. "Librarians, Information, and the 'Non-traditional' Job Market," *Canadian Journal of Information Science* 14 (1989): 12-26.

Feliciter. "New Home (and Name) for National Science Library," Ottawa: *Canadian Library Association* 20 (1974): 10-11.

Galvin, Thomas. "Convergence or Divergence in Education for the Information Professions: An Opinion Paper," *Bulletin Of the American Society for Information Science* 21 (1995): 7-12.

Gibson, Colin. "On the National Library," *Canadian Library Association Bulletin,* 5 (1948): 118-119.

Harris, Michael. *History of Libraries in the Western World.* Metuchen, N.J., Scarecrow Press, 1984.

Harris, Michael H., and Stan A. Hannah. *Into the Future: The Foundations of Library and Information Service in the Postindustrial Era.* Norwood, N.J., Ablex Publishing. p. 39, 1994.

Harris, Roma H. *Librarianship: The Erosion of a Woman's Profession.* Norwood, N.J., Ablex Publishing Corporation, 1992.

Harris, Roma, and Joanne Reid. "Career Opportunities in Library and Information Science: An Analysis of Canadian Job Advertisements in the 1980s," *Canadian Journal of Information Science* 13 (1988): 17-29.

Ink, Gary. "Book Title Output and Average Prices: 1993 Final and 1994 Preliminary Figures," in *The Bowker Annual: Library and Book Trade Almanac.* New Providence, N.J.: R. R. Bowker, 1995, pp. 510-513.

Jackson, Sidney L. *Libraries And Librarianship In The West: A Brief History.* New York, McGraw-Hill, 1974.

Johnson, Ethel. "The Special Library and Some of its Problems," *Special Libraries* 6 (1915): 158-159.

King, Donald W., Anthony Debons, Una Mansfield, and Donald L. Shirey. "A National Profile of Information Professionals," *Bulletin of the American Society for Information Science* 6 (1980): 18-22.

Kingston, Rebecca. "The National Library of Canada. A Study in the Growth of a Nation," *Canadian Library Journal* 45 (1988): 165-170.

Kochen, Manfred and Joseph C. Donahue, eds. *Information for the Community.* Chicago, American Library Association, 1976.

Lamb, William. "Canada National Library," *Encyclopedia of Library and Information Science,* Vol. 4. 1970, pp. 165-169. New York: marcel Dekker.

_____. "Towards a National Library," *Canadian Library Association Bulletin* 8 (1951): 68-71.

Lancaster, Frederick W. "Electornic Publishing," *Library Trends* 3 (1989): 316-325.

_____. "Whither Libraries? Or Wither Libraries," *College and Research Libraries* 39 (1978): 345-357. Reprinted 50 (1989):

406-419.

_____. *Libraries and Librarians in an Age of Electronics.*
Arlington, Va.: Information Resources Press, 1982.

_____. *Toward Paperless Information Systems.* New York:
Academic Press, 1978.

Large, Andrew. "Information Technology and Education for Library
and Information Studies: The Challenge," *Canadian Journal
of Information and Library Studies,* 18 (1993): 23-33.

Laribee, J. "Undergraduate and Graduate Courses in Information
Resources Management: Education and Managerial Judgement
about Appropriate Course Content," *Education for Information,*
10 (1992): 17-33.

Licklider, J. C. R. *Libraries of the Future.* Cambridge, Mass.: MIT
Press, 1965.

Machlup, Fritz. *Knowledge, Its Creation, Distribution, and Economic
Significance.* Princeton, N.J.: Princeton University Press,
1980.

Maraccacio, Kathleen Young, ed., *Gale Directory of Databases.*
Detroit: Gale Research, 1994.

Martin, William J. "Education for Information Management:
Restructuring and Reform," *Education for Information* 9
(1991): 21-28.

Mauerhoff, George. "CAN/SDI: A National SDI System in Canada,"
Libri, 1 (1974): 19-29.

McGarry, K. J. *The Changing Context of Information.* London:
Clive Bingley, 1981.

McGill University Graduate School of Library and Information Studies.
1987 Survey of Graduates. Montreal: McGill University,
1988.

154   *Librarianship and the Information Paradigm*

    18 (1993): 6-22.

Miksa, F. "Library and Information Science: Two Paradigms," in P.
    Vakkari and B. Cronin, eds., *Conceptions of Library and
    Information Science.* London: Graham Taylor, 1992, pp. 229-
    252.

Moore, Nick. *The Emerging Markets for Librarians and Information
    Workers.* London: The British Library Board, 1987.

National Library Advisory Committee. "Summary of
    Recommendations," *Canadian Library Association Bulletin* 8
    (1952): 165-166.

_____. "National Library Advisory Committee," *Canadian
    Library Association Bulletin* 6 (1950): 199.

National Library of Canada. "Annual Report 1991-1992." Ottawa:
    Supply and Services, 1992b.

_____. "The National Library of Canada's Library Development
    Centre." Ottawa: National Library of Canada, 1992a.

_____. "Music Collection." Ottawa: Supply and Services, 1991.

_____. "Annual Report 1988-1989." Ottawa: Supply and Services,
    1989b.

_____. "Publications Catalog 1989." Ottawa: Supply and
    Services, 1989a.

_____. "Library Service for Disabled Persons." Ottawa: Supply
    and Services, 1988.

_____. "Children's Literature Service." Ottawa: Supply and
    Services, 1987.

_____. "Protocol Development at the National Library of Canada." Ottawa: Supply and services, 1985.

National Research Council of Canada. "CISTI: Health Sciences Resource Centre." Ottawa: National Research Council Canada, 1986.

_____. "Fiftieth Annual Report 1966-1967." Ottawa, Public Relations Office, National Research Council of Canada, 1967.

Paris, Marion. *Library School Closing: Four Case Studies.* Metuchen, N.J.: Scarecrow Press, 1988.

Pemberton, J. Michael. *CRISTAL (Internet discussion group that is focused on library/information science education),* December 1, 1994.

Pemberton, J. Michael, and Christine R. Nugent. "Information Studies: Emergent Field, Convergent Curriculum," *Journal of Education for Library and Information Science* 36 (1995): 138.

Poster, Mark. *The Mode of Information: Poststructuralism and Social Context.* Chicago: University of Chicago Press, 1990.

Porat, Marc Uri. "Defining an Information Sector in the U.S. Economy," Report No. 15. Center for Interdisciplinary Research, Stanford University, *Information Reports and Biographies* 5 (1976): 17-31.

Roszak, Theodore. *The Cult of Information: The Folklore of Computers and the True Art of Thinking.* New York: Pantheon Books, 1986.

Rothstein, Samuel. *The Development of Reference Services, ACRL Monographs 14.* Chicago: Reference and Adult Services Division, American Library Association, 1995.

Royal Commission on National Development in the Arts, Letters and Sciences Report. Ottawa: King's Printer King's, 1951. [Massey Report]

Schrader, Alvin. "Towards a Theory of Library and Information Science," Ph.D. thesis, University of Indiana, 1983.

_____. "In Search of a Name: Information Science and its Concptual Antecedents," *Library and Information Science Research*, 6 (1984): 227-271.

_____. "The Domain of Information Science: Problems in Conceptualization and in Consensus-Building," *Information Services and Use* 6 (1986): 169-205.

Sellen, Betty-Carol, and Dimity S. Berkner. *New Options for Librarians: Finding a Job in a Related Field.* New York: Neal-Schuman, 1984.

Sigert, Lindy. Personal Interview, Halifax, February 1992.

Sineath, Timothy W., ed. *Library and Information Science Education Statistical Report.* Raleigh, N.C.: ALISE, 1995.

Stoll, Clifford. *Silicon Snake Oil: Second Thoughts on the Information Highway.* Toronto: Doubleday, 1995.

Stuart-Stubbs, Basil. *The Employment Situation for Recent Graduates of the U.B.C. School of Library, Information and Archival Studies.* Vancouver: University of British Columbia, 1985.

_____. *The Employment and Situation for Recent Graduates of the U.B.C. School of Library, Information and Archival Studies.* Vancouver: University of British Columbia, 1982.

Tague, Jean. "Information Science in Graduate Library Programs," *Canadian Library Journal* 36 (1979): 89-99.

Tague, Jean, and Jill Austin. "From Librarian to Information Scientist: Educational Directions for a Changing Profession," *Canadian Journal of Information Science* 11 (1986): 24-40.

Task Force on Program Review. "Culture and Communications: A Study Team Report to the Task Force on Program Review."

Ottawa: Supply and Services, 1986. [Nielsen Report]

Tees, Miriam. "New Roles for Library School Graduates," *Canadian Library Journal* 43 (1986): 372-376.

University of Toronto Faculty of Library and Information Science. *1987 Placement and Salary Survey.* Toronto: University of Toronto, 1988.

University of Western Ontario School of Library and Information Science. *Placement and Salary Surveys, 1983-1987.* London: University of Western Ontario.

Vagianos, Louis. "Soundings: Star-Spangled Man," *Library Journal* 97 (1972a): 2700-2701.

_____. "Information Science: A House Built on Sand," *Library Journal,* 97 (1972b): 153-157.

Vakkari, Pertti. "Library and Information Science: Its Content and Scope," in Irene P. Godden, ed., *Advances in Librarianship.* Vol. 18. Toronto: Academic Press, 1994, pp. 1-55.

Wees, Ian. *The National Library of Canada, Twenty-Five Years After.* Ottawa: Supply and Service, 1979.

_____. "The National Library of Canada, The First Quarter-Century," *Canadian Library Journal,* 35 (1978): 153-163.

Wellisch, Hans S. "Alexandrian Library," in Wayne E. Wiegand and Donald C. Davis, Jr., eds., *Encyclopedia of Library History.* New York: Garland Publishing Company, 1994, pp. 19-21.

_____. "From Information Science to Informatics: A Terminological Investigation," *Journal of Librarianship.* 33 (1972): 157-187.

Wilson, Patrick. "Bibliographic R & D," in Fritz Machlup and Una Mansfield, eds., *The Study Of Information: Interdisciplinary Messages.* New York: John Wiley, 1983, pp. 389-397.

Yuexiao, Zhang. "Definitions and Sciences of Information," *Information Processing and Management* 24 (1983): 479-491.

Index

ABOUT THE CONTRIBUTORS

Richard Apostle is a professor in the Department of Sociology and Social Anthropology at Dalhousie University. He completed a Ph.D. in sociology at the University of California (Berkeley) in 1975. He has a long-standing interest in the field of economic sociology and will be continuing his exploration of postmodernization in some new studies of library and information professions. His next project deals with the organization of special libraries and the transformation of work processes in these types of libraries.

Boris Raymond was born in 1925 of Russian parents in Harbin, China. He migrated to the United States in 1941. After serving in the Army during World War II, he returned to the University of California (Berkeley), where he took his M.A. (sociology) and M.L.S. degrees. In 1964 he joined that university's library staff as bibliographer, then served as serials librarian at the University of Nevada and assistant director (Technical Services) of libraries at the University of Manitoba, where he took an M.A. degree in history. From 1974 until his retirement from teaching in 1991, he taught library science and sociology at Dalhousie University, Halifax, Nova Scotia. He received his Ph.D. in librarianship from the University of Chicago in 1978.

Kim Adams graduated from the Masters of Library and Information Studies program at Dalhousie University in 1992. She has worked in the reference departments of several libraries and organized library collections for a number of organizations. Ms. Adams grew up in Great Village, Nova Scotia. Her writing credits include an article coauthored with Dr. Boris Raymond published in 1993 in the *Journal of Library and Information Studies*.

Paul Smith graduated from Dalhousie University in 1987 with a master's degree in sociology, concentrating in quantitative research methods and criminology. He has worked as research director on various international, national, and local surveys over the past ten years. He teaches classes in research and policing at Dalhousie University. In 1992, he was awarded a Sociology and Social Anthropology Student Society citation as best teacher of the year. Mr. Smith served with the Halifax Police Department from 1975 to 1991 and is currently employed as coordinator of Planning and Research with the Nova Scotia Department of Justice.